To Susan
With many Thanks!!
Sharon Hopper

Carolina Edens

Cherubs and other statuary accent the elaborate gardens of Middleton Place in Charleston, South Carolina.

Tulips and pansies brighten the Terrace Garden each spring at Sarah P. Duke Gardens in Durham, North Carolina.

Carolina Edens

Photographs by Al Spicer   Text by Cindy Spicer

JOHN F. BLAIR, PUBLISHER WINSTON-SALEM, NORTH CAROLINA

PRINTED AND BOUND BY R. R. DONNELLEY & SONS
DESIGNED BY DEBRA LONG HAMPTON

*The paper in this book meets the guidelines
for permanence and durability of the
Committee on Production Guidelines
for Book Longevity of the Council on
Library Resources.*

Library of Congress Cataloging-in-Publication Data
Spicer, Cindy, 1954-
     Carolina edens / photographs by Al Spicer ; text by Cindy Spicer.
         p.   cm.
     Includes bibliographical references (p.   ) and index.
     ISBN 0-89587-135-1 (alk. paper)
     1. Gardens — North Carolina.   2. Gardens — South Carolina.
  3. Gardens — North Carolina — Pictorial works.   4. Gardens — South Carolina — Pictorial works.
  I.Spicer, Al, 1950 —   .   II. Title.
  SB466.U65N7478   1995
  712'.5'09756 — dc20   95-3819

Dedication

To my parents, William and Lillian,
for instilling in me the belief that I can
accomplish anything if I give it my all.

To my sisters, Debbie and Rhonda,
two remarkable women.

Contents

ACKNOWLEDGMENTS

This book would not have been possible without the help and hard work of the countless individuals who designed and tended these gardens. These people perform a labor of love that creates beauty for all to enjoy. They spend countless hours planting, tending, and nurturing the gardens throughout the Carolinas. For their hard work and dedication, we are indebted and forever grateful. There were many people who assisted in making it possible for us to make photographs in the gardens, especially Randi Cashion, Magnolia Plantation and Gardens; Ann S. Glover, Wing Haven Gardens and Bird Sanctuary; Anna Kinsey, Brookgreen Gardens; Barbara Meeh, Elizabethan Gardens; Donna Owens, Middleton Place; Michele Raphoon, Tryon Palace and Gardens; Elizabeth Sims, Biltmore Estate; Kenneth Sprunt, Orton Plantation Gardens; Bill Steele, Daniel Stowe Botanical Garden; Gurdon Tarbox, Brookgreen Gardens; and Jean West, Boone Hall Plantation.

This project required a great deal of research, and we appreciate those who helped with the gathering of the information, especially the following individuals: Jean Ammons, Flora Macdonald Gardens; Anita Bailiff, Airlie Gardens; Amanda Barton, Hampton Park; Irvin Brawley, Davidson College; Norman L. Brunswig, Francis Beidler Forest; Sally Burrell, McKissick Museum; John Cain, New Hanover County Extension Service Arboretum; Brantley Carter, Henry Timrod Park; Rachel Cockrell, Historic Columbia Foundation; Larry T. Daniel, Sarah P. Duke Gardens; Mrs. A. J. Fletcher; Kathy Gabel, Greensboro Beautiful, Inc.; Karen Griggs, Wilkes Community College Gardens; Chris Hightower, Rose Hill Plantation State Park; Mike Hinson, Summerville Azalea Park; Chris Hughes, Mordecai Historic Park; Vivian Humphreys, Greenfield Gardens; Charlotte Jones-Roe, North Carolina Botanical Gardens; Sandy Lester, UNC Charlotte Botanical Gardens; Mrs. James T. Maynard, Hopsewee Plantation; Dr. Larry Mellichamp, UNC Charlotte Botanical Gardens; Joe Morris, Elizabeth Holmes Hurley Park; Greg Nace, Cape Fear Botanical Garden; John Palmer, Haywood Community College; Glenn Parker, Hopeland Gardens and Rye Patch; Lila Petersen, Daniel Boone Native Gardens; Mary Beth Reuter, Summerville Library; George P. Sawyer, Jr., Kalmia Gardens of Coker College; Brother Stephen, Mepkin Abbey; Louise "Scottie" Stephenson, WRAL Azalea Gardens; Preston Stockton, Reynolda Gardens of Wake Forest University; Julie C. Tovey, South Carolina Botanical Garden; Mark Towery, Swan Lake Iris Gardens; F. W. "B" Townes, Wilkes Community College Gardens; Lisa Wallace, Raleigh Municipal Rose Garden; Laura White, Hemlock Bluffs Nature Preserve; and Mrs. Herbert Wood, Garden Club of South Carolina.

We also want to thank our friends Dennis and Suzy Bridges for their support and encouragement.

Finally, we would like to thank the people at John F. Blair, Publisher, especially Carolyn Sakowski for her help and guidance, Debbie Hampton for her design and suggestions, and Andrew Waters for his patience and editing skills.

INTRODUCTION

Carolina Edens is a tour through public gardens, arboreta, and nature preserves of North and South Carolina. As the title of the book suggests, it is more than a garden guide; it's a handbook to heavenly beauty on earth. Paradise is more than the manicured neatness of a paved-path garden. It means different things to different people, and each of us holds in our heart and mind a vision of what our private Eden would be if given the opportunity to choose. Those visions assume earthly shape as gardeners strive to give substance to their visions. Whether landscaped by man, shaped entirely by nature, or formed by a cooperative effort between the two, the gardens of North and South Carolina are as varied as the gardeners who tend them. Some gardens included in the book are indeed paved, immaculately manicured, and considered grand and elegantly impressive on any scale. The magnificence of these gardens echoes the power nature and wealth can wield on an empty landscape. There are, however, other gardens tucked in out-of-the-way places which may remind you of your own backyard bramble or your grandmother's kitchen garden where, as a child, you played with the neighbor's cat. These gardens possess a simple elegance which speaks eloquently to the soul of gardeners determined to shape their own personal Eden. There is something for everyone.

The photographs in this book do more than record the fresh-faced flowers before sun and time fade their delicate petals. They capture the essence of nature's timeless cycle of life, as seen in the exuberant flush of spring blooms and the ever-changing landscape man diligently tries to contain. The welcome colors of spring and the vibrant hues of autumn are instrumental in luring you into the gardens, catching your eye, and holding your imagination. Nature's palette of vivid colors is captured and displayed in these photographs to enable you to experience the garden and feel as though you are there. Take the feeling one step further and use this book to turn the feeling into the reality of a visit.

Easy to use, this book is divided into two parts, North Carolina and South Carolina. All gardens are listed alphabetically by city. Each garden within a city is given an address. This address is provided as a source for obtaining more information and is not necessarily the location of the garden. A short history of the garden sets the stage for your visit, and information, such as hours and fees, is included to help plan your visit. Outstanding garden collections or noteworthy plantings are highlighted in the features section. The tips section offers information about facilities associated with the garden and observations which will hopefully make for an enjoyable visit. Directions to each garden begin from the nearest interstate or state highway and are as specific as possible. However, always obtain a current map to assist you in your trip. Along with your maps, remember to take the book with you. On your garden travels jot down personal notes about new plants you would like to grow or new varieties of your favorite plant. Turn down the corner of a page and make the book your own. Allow yourself to be led, eyes wide open, down the garden path, as you personally experience Carolina's Edens.

Carolina Edens

North Carolina

Tryon Palace garden in New Bern

Biltmore Estate

One North Pack Square
Asheville, North Carolina 28801-3122
800-543-2961   or   704-255-1700

HISTORY

*B*iltmore Estate gardens are as richly appointed as the mansion George Washington Vanderbilt called home. Designed by Frederick Law Olmsted, the father of American landscape architecture and designer of New York's Central Park, Biltmore's gardens can be listed among the finest examples of landscape design.

In the 1880s, Olmsted was commissioned to provide garden grandeur equal to the structure that was to be Biltmore House, the largest private residence ever to be built in America. He met the challenge supremely with diverse native plantings, tradition based on centuries of European garden design, and touches of Victorian elegance and grace.

The three-mile approach road where nature's wild hand and man's ordered plan come together is a testament to Olmsted's genius. The tree-lined approach road curves to allow the estate to unfold slowly as you move closer to Biltmore House. Once at the house, you are immediately struck by the grand scale of everything. Biltmore House is truly magnificent. It is difficult to imagine anything else quite so grand, until your eyes behold the gardens.

The gardens do not pale when compared to the house; because of Olmsted's training and naturalistic vision, the gardens become an impressive extension of the house. He incorporated English traditional and European pastoral designs into the already plentiful native flora to provide a legacy of beauty for many generations to come.

HOURS

Daily, 9:00 a.m. to 5:00 p.m.
Closed Thanksgiving,
Christmas, and New Year's Day
Biltmore Estate Evenings 6:30 p.m. to 9:00 p.m.,
Fridays and Saturdays beginning in July
and continuing until September

Call for a special events brochure.
Events include a Festival of Flowers and Biltmore by Candlelight (reservations suggested)

FEE

Children nine and under are admitted free with paying adult. Handicapped visitors receive admission discounts.

Statues enhance the gardens throughout the estate.

salvia, dahlias, and zinnias. Fall is time for chrysanthemums, which flourish until heavy frost.

Roses, also, have a home in this garden, which features All-American Rose Selections and at least three thousand roses of different varieties. A conservatory and greenhouses lie beyond the rose garden and provide the rest of Biltmore with cut flowers and bedding plants.

On the other side of the conservatory lies the Azalea Garden, which by all accounts boasts the world's most complete collection of native azaleas. Just down the path from the Azalea Garden is the Bass Pond with a boathouse and gazebo.

SIZE

75 acres of landscaped gardens

FEATURES

The Italian Garden, featuring three reflecting pools planted with various aquatic plants and bordered by sculptures, is adjacent to the house. The shrub garden, known as "The Ramble," leads from the Italian Garden to the four-acre Walled English Garden. This true English flower garden is often described by garden critics as "the finest English garden in America." Beds inside the walls are planted three times a year. In fall approximately fifty thousand tulip bulbs are planted, followed by plantings of summer annuals including marigolds,

DIRECTIONS

From I-40 take Exit 50 or 50B and follow the signs. The Biltmore Estate is on NC 25 just north of the exits.

TIPS

The expansive gardens at Biltmore Estate can be a lot to tour in one day, so come prepared to walk. Wear comfortable shoes and allow ample time, approximately four to five hours, for proper touring of the gardens. Give yourself occasional rest stops at any of the strategically located benches, enjoy a delicious lunch at the Stable Cafe, or brown-bag it with your favorites from home. Plan a visit to the gift shops and give yourself plenty of time to photograph the beauty and splendor of the Biltmore gardens. Handicapped facilities are available.

Another dawn arrives in the Italian Garden at the Biltmore Estate.
The gardens on the estate are a testament to the genius of Frederick Law Olmsted.

Biltmore's collection of native azaleas is one of the finest in the United States.

The conservatory, designed by Biltmore architect Richard Morris Hunt, is surrounded by more than fifty thousand tulips which bloom each spring.

Magnificent is the word most often used to describe the Biltmore House; however, the scale and design of the gardens warrant the same description. The gardens, as richly decorated as the house, change their color and texture as the seasons progress. In early spring, tulips, azaleas, and dogwoods supply a profuse display of color. Summertime displays of dahlias, cannas, zinnias, marigolds, and salvia brighten the landscape. As the growing season comes to a close, chrysanthemums and autumn leaves carry the gardens into winter.

Tulips provide color inside the Walled English Garden.

*A rustic bridge allows garden visitors to cross a stream
which winds through the Azalea Garden and Arboretum.*

Botanical Gardens at Asheville

151 W. T. Weaver Boulevard
Asheville, North Carolina 28804-3414
704-252-5190

HISTORY

The Botanical Gardens at Asheville were organized and planted with one thing in mind: to showcase and preserve plants native to the Southern Appalachian Mountains. Noted for their collection of plants unique to North Carolina, the gardens were organized in 1960 by the Asheville Garden Club and designed by landscape architect Doan Ogden.

HOURS

Daily, sunrise to sunset

FEE

None

SIZE

10 acres along Reed Creek

FEATURES

Plants native to North Carolina, the Blue Ridge, and Southern Appalachian Mountains are the focus of these well-planted gardens. Spring is, of course, the best time to visit the Botanical Gardens at Asheville; however, there is always something in bud or bloom, and seasonal displays of leaves and fruits are always attractive.

DIRECTIONS

From I-240 take US 19/23/70 Exit 4B. Travel about two miles to the exit for NC 251, turn right at the end of the ramp onto Broadway Street. W. T. Weaver Boulevard will be on the left at about 0.5 mile. The garden entrance is on the left at the corner of Broadway Street and W. T. Weaver Boulevard.

TIPS

Many events dealing with conservation and botany are sponsored by the gardens, so call ahead. Some popular events are the annual Day in the Gardens and the Annual Wildflower Pilgrimage. The Annual Wildflower Pilgrimage, co-sponsored by the University of North Carolina at Asheville and Blue Ridge Parkway, is a three-day event usually beginning on the Friday before the first Saturday in May. Access is limited for the handicapped.

A nursery web spider makes itself at home on a black-eyed Susan.

Footbridge to the gardens leads to a closer inspection of flowers and plants growing along Reed Creek.

Craggy Gardens

Blue Ridge Parkway
200 BB&T Building
One Pack Square
Asheville, North Carolina 28801-3123
704-298-0398

HISTORY

*G*reat Craggy Mountains, known locally as the Craggy Gardens, are an area of exposed balds which provide excellent views of the Southern Appalachian Mountains. Craggy Gardens are, in fact, natural gardens consisting of native Catawba rhododendron. Before the Blue Ridge Parkway was established, settlers pastured their livestock on these balds during the summer months, effectively keeping them clear. All grazing was stopped, however, in 1950 when the land was acquired for the Blue Ridge Parkway. Removal of domestic livestock allowed the native flora to return and flourish.

HOURS

Daily, sunrise to sunset

FEE

None

SIZE

700 acres

FEATURES

A network of trails, some self-guided, lead to gorgeous vistas of the surrounding Black and Appalachian mountains, waterfalls, picnic area, and visitor center. Native plants, particularly the Catawba rhododendron and flame azalea, abound in these natural gardens.

DIRECTIONS

From I-40 in Asheville go north on the Blue Ridge Parkway to Milepost 364.

TIPS

This area, designated as a Natural Heritage Area, has extremes in elevation and terrain, so bring suitable shoes and clothing. Early to mid-June is the best time for rhododendron and azalea blooms. Native wildflowers bloom at other times throughout the summer months. The visitor center, exhibits, and restrooms are handicapped accessible.

The North Carolina Arboretum

P. O. Box 6617
Asheville, North Carolina   28816-6617
704-665-2492

HISTORY

*N*orth Carolina's general assembly established the "Western North Carolina Arboretum" in 1986 as a research and conservation facility of the North Carolina University system. In 1989, the name was changed to "The North Carolina Arboretum" in order to more accurately describe the institution's contribution to the entire state through programs in research, conservation, education, and landscape development. The arboretum, located within the Bent Creek Experimental Forest of the Pisgah National Forest, was established to provide a positive influence on all institutions and individuals through responsible use of our natural resources.

HOURS

Monday through Friday
8:00 a.m. to 4:30 p.m.

FEE

None

SIZE

424 acres

FEATURES

This is a very young arboretum with lots of plans for the future; however, quite a lot of things have already been accomplished. The master plan calls for a Visitor Education Center, Orientation Complex, demonstration gardens and greenhouses, Synoptic Terrace Garden, Core and Water gardens, an Ethnobotanical Center, and a Horticultural Therapy Barrier-free Garden for the handicapped.

DIRECTIONS

From I-26 take Exit 2 (NC 191) and turn right. At approximately 2 miles turn right onto Bent Creek Ranch Road. Travel about 0.3 mile to a fork in the road, take the left fork, Wesley Branch Road, and the arboretum entrance will be on the left at approximately 1 mile. Once inside, make a turn to the left towards the Visitor Education Center.

TIPS

The staff members conduct various nature and environmental programs at the arboretum, so write or call for details. Exhibits are handicapped accessible.

Daniel Stowe Botanical Garden

6500 South New Hope Road
Belmont, North Carolina   28012-9906
704-825-4490

HISTORY

Originally a trading ground for the Catawba and Cherokee Indians located along the North and South Carolina border, the garden is named for retired textile executive Daniel Stowe. Stowe chartered the Daniel Jonathan Stowe Conservancy in 1989. The conservancy, whose motto is "A Partnership with Nature," intends to create a world-class garden rivaling the more established United States gardens.

   The master plan for this young garden will utilize more than four hundred acres along the Catawba Creek near Lake Wylie. The first phase of the plan, designed by Geoffrey Rausch, will be to develop one quarter of the garden by cleverly incorporating buildings, water features, and additional plantings of imported species into the existing flora. Display gardens and conservatories will offer an opportunity to gain an awareness of and an appreciation for the diversity our planet offers.

HOURS

Monday through Saturday
9:00 a.m. to 5:00 p.m.
Sunday
12:00 p.m. to 5:00 p.m.
Closed Christmas Day

FEE

None

SIZE

400 acres

FEATURES

   At present, the interim garden covers about ten acres, three of which are beautifully landscaped with perennials. The remaining seven acres display plantings of lilies, seasonal annuals, and a kitchen garden. All of the grounds surrounding the visitor center, the education center, and gift shop are exquisitely landscaped with native plants and shrubs.

The gift-shop porch offers the visitor a panoramic view of the garden as well as a comfortable place to sit.

DIRECTIONS

From I-85 North take the exit for New Hope Road and turn right onto New Hope Road. At 11 miles the garden will be on the right. From I-85 South take Exit 26 (Belmont Abbey College), and turn right onto North Main Street which becomes South Main Street and then Armstrong Ford Road. At 6.2 miles, turn left onto New Hope Road. The garden will be on the right at 9 miles.

TIPS

Any time is a good time to visit, as particular care has been taken with the perennial garden in order to provide seasonal color and texture. Of course, spring and summer offer the best variety of blooms. The handicapped visitor is accommodated with parking, ramps, and other facilities. Call or write the garden for information on educational programs and updates on progress.

Daniel Boone Native Gardens

P.O. Box 2885
Boone, North Carolina   28607-2885
704-264-6390   or   704-264-7181

HISTORY

*N*amed for America's most beloved frontiersman, the Daniel Boone Native Gardens are among the pioneer gardens in the Southeast for their dedication to preserving native flora. The gardens opened in May 1967; but, the idea for them occurred ten years earlier in response to a lament from eminent landscape architect H. Stuart Ortloff. While at a flower-show school sponsored by the Garden Club of North Carolina, Ortloff expressed his dismay at the difficulty encountered in studying native plants. He recommended that an area, easily accessible to the public, be set aside for their study. Members of the club acted upon his recommendation, and in 1959, they adopted such a garden as their project. Doan Ogden of Asheville was selected as garden architect.

When the time came for the gardens to be planted, clubs from across the state were encouraged to send plants representative of their area. These plants enhanced the natural landscaping and increased the diversity of plants available for study.

HOURS

Daily, 9:00 a.m. to 6:00 p.m.
May through October
Weather permitting

FEE

Yes, some discounts apply

SIZE

10 acres

FEATURES

An extensive collection of native plants and wildflowers is gathered for education and preservation. The gardens offer specimens of native azaleas, pink and white dogwoods, and a very old black mountain heart cherry. Grassy allées, bordered with other native plants and wild perennials, entice visitors toward other garden features, including a bog garden, fern garden, meditation garden, and rustic gazebo. Also featured is Squire Boone's hand-hewn log cabin.

DIRECTIONS

The gardens are located on Horn in the West Drive in Daniel Boone Park, just off US 421/321 and US 221/NC 105 Extension. There are directional signs.

The time to visit these gardens is in early spring when the azaleas are blooming. Make sure to bring a sweater, as the springtime temperatures can be quite changeable. Access is limited for handicapped visitors.

Bur marigolds and wild geraniums are common North Carolina wildflowers.

Hemlock Bluffs Nature Preserve

2616 Kildaire Farm Road
Cary, North Carolina   27511-9612
919-378-5980

HISTORY

*T*hanks to a concerned group of Cary citizens, Hemlock Bluffs Nature Preserve is a wild haven in the midst of concrete and asphalt. In 1976, the citizens successfully lobbied the state government to have the property declared a nature preserve. The preserve remained unmanaged until 1989, when interest was rekindled and the city, in cooperation with the state, took action to manage and staff the preserve.

HOURS

Preserve
Daily, 9:00 a.m. to sunset

Nature Center
Monday through Saturday
10:00 a.m. to 7:00 p.m.
May through September

Monday through Saturday
10:00 a.m. to 5:00 p.m.
October through April
Sunday
1:00 p.m. to 5:00 p.m.
Year round

FEE

None

SIZE

150 acres

FEATURES

Four-hundred-year-old Canadian hemlocks and other plants normally found in mountainous climes are the main attractions; but, they are by no means the only things to see. A system of well-maintained trails and overlooks provide easy access to scenic areas of the preserve. Wildflower enthusiasts will delight in the Native Wildflower Garden located behind the Stevens Nature

A daddy-long-legs strolls across Velvet-foot mushrooms.

Center. There is an array of native plants blooming at the preserve from February through October.

DIRECTIONS

From I-40 take Exit 287 (Cary-Harrison Avenue) towards Cary proper. From the exit, turn left at 2.4 miles onto Maynard Loop Road. Continue 4.2 miles and turn left onto Kildaire Farm Road. The preserve is on the right at 3.6 miles.

TIPS

The staff at Hemlock Bluffs Nature Preserve is very ecologically minded. A variety of guided tours, nature walks, and interactive displays encourage visitors to participate in the exploration and preservation of our environment. The Stevens Nature Center is closed on all town holidays. The nature center and Native Wildflower Garden are handicapped accessible.

Coker Arboretum

Campus Box 3375, Totten Center
University of North Carolina at Chapel Hill
Chapel Hill, North Carolina 27599-3375
919-962-0522

HISTORY

Once a boggy cow pasture belonging to Professor Eben Alexander, the Coker Arboretum began humbly in the early 1920s. Professor William Coker, the University of North Carolina's first professor of botany, believed the old pasture would be the perfect place to plant and preserve trees, shrubs, and vines native to North Carolina. It would also serve as an outdoor classroom for his students. Over the next twenty years, Professor Coker imported and planted many ornamental plants, shrubs, and trees related to native species in order to round out the arboretum's collection. At present, there are approximately 580 species of trees and shrubs in the landscape which is colorfully complemented by seasonal plantings of annuals and perennials.

At one of the many gates leading into the arboretum, there is a plaque, covered with the patina of age, a bit of moss, and some overgrown plants, which recalls the sentiments of thousands of students: "A collection of native and ornamental trees and shrubs begun in 1903 by Professor William Coker (1872-1953) for the enjoyment and education of all generations of university students." This is how the Class of 1967 remembered Professor Coker for the legacy of the arboretum.

HOURS

Daily, sunrise to sunset

FEE

None

SIZE

5 acres

FEATURES

The character and charm of the arboretum is enhanced by the surroundings, the university's campus. Bordered on two sides by old, moss-covered stone walls, the garden offers benches, brick and sandy footpaths, an old greenhouse, and a wisteria arbor that runs the entire length of one side. Animal life abounds inside the arboretum, with chipmunks, rabbits, birds, and squirrels.

Purple and white coneflowers are among the many perennials at the Coker Arboretum.

DIRECTIONS

From I-40 take NC 86 South 4 miles to East Franklin Street. Turn left onto East Franklin Street and go 3 blocks to Morehead Planetarium and Rose Garden on the right. The arboretum is adjacent to the planetarium and directly behind the Chapel of the Cross Episcopal Parish. Metered parking is available at the planetarium.

TIPS

Birds abound in the arboretum, so bring your binoculars and your bird book. Also, it's a good idea to arrive early if you plan to park at the planetarium, as spaces fill up quickly. Handicapped parking is available at the planetarium; however, sections of the garden may not be readily accessible to the handicapped.

The gazebo at the Gene Strowd Community Rose Garden is surrounded by a profusion of blooms.

Gene Strowd Community Rose Garden

Chapel Hill Community Center
120 South Estes Drive
Chapel Hill, North Carolina 27514 -2880
919-968-2784

HISTORY

*D*edicated September 30, 1990, in honor of Fletcher Eugene Strowd, a founding member of the Chapel Hill Rose Society, the rose garden was a joint project between the society and the town's parks and recreation department. In 1987, a partnership was forged between the two, and the rose garden was no longer only an idea. The garden was planned by Mr. Strowd, who had a hand in planting several hundred of the garden's six hundred roses during its construction. Mr. Strowd was the primary caretaker until his death in 1991.

HOURS

Daily, sunrise to sunset

FEE

None

SIZE

½ acre with approximately six hundred rose bushes

FEATURES

The diamond-shaped garden features an entry bower covered in climbing roses. A split-rail fence provides support for climbers and ramblers, and a gazebo, located directly across from the entrance, gives the garden visitor a shady spot to read or have lunch. Adjacent to the garden is "The Learning Garden," a small, but abundantly planted, garden of annuals and perennials. This garden, like the Strowd garden, is the result of a cooperative effort, this one between the parks and recreation department and the North Carolina Botanical Garden.

DIRECTIONS

From I-40 take US 15/501 Bypass South to Estes Drive. Turn right and go 0.5 mile; the Chapel Hill Community Center will be on the left.

TIPS

This garden is small and could be toured in conjunction with other gardens in the Chapel Hill area. Handicapped parking is available at the community center, and the garden is handicapped accessible.

North Carolina Botanical Garden

Campus Box 3375, Totten Center
University of North Carolina at Chapel Hill
Chapel Hill, North Carolina 27599-3375
919-962-0522

HISTORY

Born from a desire for beauty and maintained to further public awareness of nature's treasures, the North Carolina Botanical Garden began quite innocently in 1903. Francis Venable, president of the University of North Carolina, enlisted the aid of Professor William Coker to improve a soggy piece of ground on campus. Professor Coker began his work and was soon joined by a colleague, Professor Henry Totten. On Professor Coker's soggy site, Professor Totten developed a medicinal garden to use in teaching his medical and pharmacy students the important role of plants in medicine.

As the years passed, the two professors outgrew the outdoor classroom, so in the late 1920s they began working to expand and relocate their garden. The plan, according to Professor Coker, was to collect specimens of "all the trees and shrubs in North Carolina" and find a proper place to plant them. At first, a vacant piece of university property housed the ever-expanding collections acquired during the 1930s and 1940s, but more room was needed.

In 1952, the university's trustees approved the creation of a botanical garden and set aside seventy-two acres of woodland. Over the years, more land has been added, either through donations or university acquisitions, to make the arboretum a more beautiful garden.

HOURS

Daily, 8:00 a.m. to 5:00 p.m.
Mid-March through November
Weekdays, 8:00 a.m. to 5:00 p.m.
Winter

FEE

None

SIZE

600 acres

FEATURES

This garden, the largest natural botanical garden in the southeastern United States, serves as a regional center for conservation and research of plants native to the Southeast. One will find plants having special botanical

Praying mantis sits atop a yellow trumpet plant watching for the next meal.

interest and plants which are either threatened or endangered. The North Carolina Botanical Garden includes nature trails, the Mason Farm Biological Reserve (a permit is required), Coker Pinetum, Coker Arboretum (a separate listing is included on page 22), and the William L. Hunt Arboretum. The Totten Center features collections of native plants, assorted wildflowers, ferns, carnivorous and aquatic plants, and herbs. Guided tours are available with advance notice for groups of ten to sixty. Self-guided tour pamphlets are available at the center.

A six-spotted fishing spider perches on a lily pad.

Native water lilies bloom in the aquatic garden.

DIRECTIONS

From I-40 take US 15/501 Bypass South (Fordham Boulevard) 4 miles. Then, turn left onto Old Mason Farm Road. The garden is on the corner.

TIPS

Blooming schedules are provided at the garden, as are other pamphlets designed to assist and educate the gardening public. If you plan to hike the nature trails allow thirty-five to forty-five minutes for the Streamside Trail (⅓ mile) and forty-five to sixty minutes for the Oak-Hickory Trail (1 mile). Gardening questions can be called in each weekday between 12:00 p.m. and 1:00 p.m. Handicapped parking is available; however, sections of the garden may present problems for the handicapped.

UNC Charlotte Botanical Gardens

Department of Biology
UNC Charlotte
Charlotte, North Carolina   28223-0002
704-547-2555   or   704-547-2364

HISTORY

*G*ardens are usually a reflection of the interests of their gardener, and the UNC Charlotte Botanical Gardens are no exception. Established in stages with many benefactors, the gardens were started in 1966 with the development of the Van Landingham Glen. The glen, named for Ralph Van Landingham, an avid rhododendron grower, was followed in 1979 by the Susie Harwood Garden, named for Mr. Van Landingham's mother. The Harwood Garden was soon followed by the McMillan Greenhouses in 1983. A gift from Dr. Thomas and Dorothy McMillan and the Schoenith Foundation made the construction of the greenhouses a reality.

HOURS

Gardens
Daily, sunrise to sunset

Greenhouses
Monday through Friday
9:00 a.m. to 4:00 p.m.
Saturdays
10:00 a.m. to 3:00 p.m.

FEE

None

SIZE

10 acres

FEATURES

The Van Landingham Glen and the Susie Harwood Garden are two distinctly different gardens. The four-thousand-square-foot greenhouses feature five different growing environments.

DIRECTIONS

From I-85 take Exit 45A (East Harris Boulevard). Go 1.5 miles to University City Boulevard (NC 49) exit and turn left. At 1 mile turn left into UNC Charlotte. Wind around about 0.2 mile on Mary Alexander Road. The greenhouses are on the left, and the gardens are on the right.

Spring mornings are good times to visit the gardens as they provide a haven for several species of birds. The Susie Harwood Garden, with its exotic varieties, is especially nice. Parking is available at the greenhouses. The rolling terrain may be difficult for the handicapped.

Green frogs add to the sounds encountered at the garden.

The Susie Harwood Garden's moon gate entrance.

Wing Haven Gardens and Bird Sanctuary

248 Ridgewood Avenue
Charlotte, North Carolina 28209-1632
704-334-0664

HISTORY

Wing Haven, home to Elizabeth and Edwin Clarkson from 1927 to 1988, is a wonderful little "wilderness" encircled by a brick wall and situated in a beautiful old Charlotte neighborhood. In 1927, the Clarksons moved into the home to begin their married life. Since the house was constructed on the treeless red-clay lot, Elizabeth began planning and planting the garden almost immediately. Gardening was a passion for the Clarksons; however, an orphaned bluebird they named Tommy added another dimension to their hobby.

Elizabeth raised Tommy after his mother was killed by a hawk. He was special to Elizabeth, and she provided him with food and shelter. Tommy "lived" with the Clarksons for eight years and was allowed the run of the house. He came and went as he pleased through a hole cut in an upstairs window sash. The Clarksons derived so much pleasure from little Tommy, they allowed other birds, and even a rabbit, access to their home.

In 1970, Wing Haven was given to the Wing Haven Foundation which had been established by friends and relatives of the Clarksons to insure the preservation of this tiny wilderness.

HOURS
Tuesday and Wednesday
3:00 p.m. to 5:00 p.m.
Sunday
2:00 p.m. to 5:00 p.m.

FEE
None

SIZE
3½ acres in a residential section

FEATURES

Wing Haven was definitely designed for the birds and has been planted to provide cover, shelter, and nesting sights for our feathered friends. Birdbaths and fountains attract birds and provide soothing natural music for the human visitor. Other features include a formal garden, a rose garden, and a woodland garden planted with a variety of blooming plants, shrubs, and trees. Ornamental plaques, statues, and benches located throughout the garden provide thoughtful diversions for all.

Boxwoods border the classically designed herb garden.

Male house finch, one of the many species of birds that visit or call Wing Haven home.

DIRECTIONS

From I-77 take Exit 6A (Woodlawn Road) and travel 3 miles to Park Road. Turn left onto Park Road and at 0.5 mile, turn right onto Hillside Avenue. Go to the four-way stop sign at Westfield Road and turn left. Go one block to Ridgewood Avenue and turn right.

The Grapevine Path and Main Garden are among the many features that add to Wing Haven's quaint charm.

TIPS

Don't let the limited hours prevent you from visiting Wing Haven. Take time to watch the twelve-minute video, "Wing Haven: A Gift to the City," as it sets the stage for a meaningful visit. Brick pathways can be slippery and handicapped accessibility is limited. Parties of five or more should call for a tour.

Tanglewood Arboretum and Rose Garden

P.O. Box 1040
Clemmons, North Carolina 27012-1040
910-766-0591

HISTORY

Tanglewood was an appropriate name for the farm Margaret Griffith shared with her husband and children in the early 1900s. For Margaret, the gnarled underbrush along the Yadkin River, which ran through the farm, recreated the settings in Nathaniel Hawthorne's, *Tanglewood Tales*. The name was so fitting that William Neal Reynolds kept it when he purchased the property from the Griffith family in 1921. Thirty years later, Tanglewood, no longer the tangled woodland of its early years, was left to the citizens of Forsyth County by William Neal Reynolds.

The beauty of Tanglewood is enhanced by the landscape handiwork of Frank Lustig, the gardener for the Reynolds family. His plantings, many imported from around the world, can still be found in the arboretum.

HOURS

Daily, 8:00 a.m. to dusk

Accommodations are accessible twenty-four hours a day and rented shelters are open past posted hours.

FEE

Parking fee

SIZE

1200 acres on the Yadkin River

FEATURES

There is something for everyone at this exceptional county park. For the botanically inclined, the rose garden is located at the front of the manor house, and the botanical gardens are located at the rear. The area around the house is the arboretum, home to some impressive specimens of oak and black walnut. There is also a fragrance garden which appeals to several species of butterfly.

If flora isn't what you fancy, you can enjoy several other pastimes during the year. In early spring, the Tanglewood Steeplechase attracts horse lovers from everywhere. There is a summer music series presented by the Winston-Salem Symphony, and the Festival of Lights has become a Tanglewood winter tradition.

Touch of Class and other All-American Rose Selections winners are featured in the rose garden.

DIRECTIONS

From I-40 take Exit 184 (Lewisville-Clemmons Road), turn left (south) and go approximately 1 mile to US 158. Turn right and travel 1.2 miles (crossing Harper Road), the park entrance will be on the left.

TIPS

Home to the Vantage Championship on the Senior PGA Tour, golf is king at Tanglewood so bring the clubs. Don't forget the canoe, the saddle, and the hiking boots either. Most of the facilities are handicapped accessible.

Campus Arboretum of Haywood Community College

Freelander Drive
Clyde, North Carolina 28721-9453
704-627-2821 or 704-627-4640

HISTORY

*P*reserving the natural resources and beautifying the campus of Haywood Community College was a concern of the board of trustees when the college moved to its present location in 1970. The site, originally a farm, gave landscape architect Doan Ogden of Asheville a myriad of natural features with which to work. One of the features was a large oak forest containing trees over a hundred years old. Ogden's plan called for the preservation of a large section of the oak forest, which is now the core of the arboretum.

In 1977, a concerned group of trustees led the push to have the campus grounds and the forest designated as an official arboretum. Since its inception, the arboretum has served many of the college's students as their living classroom by providing them the unique opportunity to experience, from a hands-on perspective, the intricacies of the ecological system and the important role plants play.

HOURS

Monday through Saturday
8:00 a.m. to 10:00 p.m.

FEE

None

SIZE

80 acres

FEATURES

One of the highlights of this arboretum is the one-acre Rhododendron Garden, bordering a winding pathway through a wooded area between campus buildings. Other plants such as roses, conifers, and assorted perennials are showcased in special display gardens located throughout the campus. Also of special interest is the oak forest, a pond, and a mill house.

Cleome and other perennials accent the landscape at Campus Arboretum.

DIRECTIONS

From I-40 take Exit 27 onto US 19/23/74. Exit the highway almost immediately at Exit 107 (Jones Cove Road). Turn left at the end of the ramp and go under the bridge. The entrance to Haywood Community College is just to the left of the underpass.

TIPS

The layout of the Rhododendron Garden is especially well-designed and offers the visitor and student a place for quiet reflection. Tours can be arranged by calling ahead or writing the arboretum director. Handicapped accessibility to some sections of the arboretum is limited.

Davidson College Arboretum

P.O. Box 1748, Davidson College
Davidson, North Carolina 28036-1748
704-892-2119 or 704-892-2596

HISTORY

*I*n 1869, the Davidson College Board of Trustees recognized the importance of preserving the natural surroundings of the campus. They envisioned a campus which, by its content, would represent the forest growth and botany of the region. Steps were taken to protect and maintain existing flora, and over the years, various trees and shrubs, native and imported, were added to the campus which was fast becoming an unofficial arboretum.

In the early 1980s, Davidson president, Samuel R. Spencer, Jr., was approached by Henry M. Cathey, the director of the National Arboretum in Washington, D.C. Cathey urged Dr. Spencer to seek official status for the campus as a working arboretum and offered his support. In 1982, the campus was officially designated as an arboretum. Cathey's encouragement and the financial support of private and corporate donors made the arboretum a reality.

HOURS

Daily, sunrise to sunset

FEE

None

SIZE

85 acres of the campus

FEATURES

The campus boasts an excellent collection of native trees on beautifully maintained grounds. Plants are well labeled to assist the visitor with identification. It is also important to note the grounds are maintained using the principles of organic gardening.

DIRECTIONS

From I-77 take Exit 30 and go east, away from Lake Norman, on Griffith Street. At 1.1 miles the road will end at the campus.

TIPS

The college offers a tree tour map which is available by writing or calling the Associate Director of Buildings and Grounds. Paved walkways afford nearly unlimited access to the handicapped.

Penny's Bend Nature Preserve

Campus Box 3375, Totten Center
University of North Carolina at Chapel Hill
Chapel Hill, North Carolina 27599-3375
919-962-0522

HISTORY

*I*n 1890, D. G. McDuffie was hired to survey properties belonging to Paul Cameron located along the Eno River. When the survey was finished, a prominent bend in the river within Snow Hill Plantation was labeled "Penny's Bend." No one knows how the bend got its name, in all probability a family by that name owned the property before the Camerons built a grist mill there in 1836. The mill was eventually destroyed by floods. The property, now owned by the United States Army Corps of Engineers, is managed by the North Carolina Botanical Garden through a cooperative agreement.

HOURS

Daily, sunrise to sunset

FEE

None

SIZE

84 acres along the Eno River

FEATURES

Spring wildflowers such as Dutchman's-breeches, blue wild indigo, hoary puccoon, and trout lilies can all be found along the banks of the Eno River. Penny's Bend also serves as a wildflower "nursery" where uncommon and rare species are propagated for re-introduction into other protected areas.

DIRECTIONS

From I-85 take the US 501 North Exit (Duke Street/Roxboro) and travel 0.5 mile to West Murray Avenue and turn right. At 0.9 mile, turn left onto North Roxboro Street. Travel 0.4 mile and turn right onto Old Oxford Road (SR 1004). Cross the Eno River at 3.1 miles and turn left on Snow Hill Road (SR 1631). Parking for the preserve is at the intersection.

TIPS

This is a wilderness area and not equipped with facilities. Wear hiking boots and bring insect repellent for summer visits. The preserve borders private property, so pay attention to the trail markers and boundary lines. The area is not handicapped accessible.

Sarah P. Duke Gardens

Duke University
Durham, North Carolina 27706-7706
919-684-3698

HISTORY

*O*riginally planned to be accessible only to students and faculty members of Duke University, today the Sarah P. Duke Gardens host more than two hundred thousand visitors each year. The initial plan for the garden was the brainchild of Dr. Frederic Hanes of Duke Hospital and was financed by Sarah P. Duke, wife of Benjamin Duke, one of the founders of the university. The Terrace Garden, commonly called the Terraces, was commissioned by Mary Duke Biddle to memorialize her mother Sarah P. Duke. It was designed in the late 1930s by Ellen Shipman.

The gardens, officially opened to the public in 1934, have evolved into quite an impressive collection of formal and informal gardens, each separately designed by leading landscape architects and designers such as Ellen Shipman, Frederic Leubuscher, William B. S. Leong, Richard H. Fillmore, and Linda Jewell.

HOURS

Daily, 8:00 a.m. to sunset

FEE

None

SIZE

55 acres

FEATURES

The fifty-five acres of the gardens consist of twenty acres of developed gardens and thirty-five acres of pine forest which are destined to become the Asiatic Arboretum. The arboretum is planted with trees and shrubs native to the Far East. Gardens offering various other delights comprise the remaining twenty acres. When entering the gardens at the main entrance on Anderson Street, you are first met by the Rose Garden. Over three hundred bushes grace the circular entrance and set the stage for your visit to either the Asiatic Arboretum or the developed gardens to the left.

The focal point of the gardens is the Terrace Garden, which is planted with bulbs and seasonal annuals. Highlighting the Terraces is the magnificent pergola covered with wisteria. The H. L. Blomquist Garden of Native Plants, just off the Azalea Court Allée, is home to an extensive collection of native wildflowers containing more than 850 species and varieties. Adding to the diversity of the gardens are representations of an alpine meadow, a rock garden, the Hanes Iris Garden, and the Azalea Court.

A pergola, covered with Japanese wisteria, is the main focus of the Terrace Garden designed by Ellen Shipman.

DIRECTIONS

From I-85 take Exit 175 (US 15/501 Bypass) and at 1.5 miles take the NC 751 exit. Turn left at the end of the ramp and at 0.9 mile turn left onto Duke University Road. Travel 0.8 mile and turn left onto Anderson Street. The gardens will be on the left at 0.2 mile.

TIPS

It is easy to spend the day at these wonderfully diverse gardens. Regardless of your particular horticultural interest you'll find it represented at the Sarah P. Duke Gardens. Parking, during the week, is limited to the Anderson Street parking lot; however, on weekends campus parking areas can be used by the public. A semi-annual newsletter of events and information is published by the gardens and can be obtained by sending a post-card with your name and address to the gardens. The handicapped visitor may need assistance, most areas of the gardens are accessible with varying degrees of difficulty.

Tulips, underplanted with pansies, signify the arrival of spring at the Sarah P. Duke Gardens.

Benches are scattered along walkways throughout Sarah P. Duke Gardens.

Cape Fear Botanical Garden

536 North Eastern Boulevard
Fayetteville, North Carolina 28301-5100
910-486-0221

HISTORY

In 1989, a group of Fayetteville gardening enthusiasts formed the Friends of the Botanical Garden in response to their city's need for a public garden. Their primary goal was to secure and develop a property suitable to support and display plants native to the Cape Fear region of North Carolina. This young garden, located along the bluffs of the Cape Fear River and Cross Creek, is truly a joint effort. Beginning with a gift of property from the city of Fayetteville, Cape Fear Botanical Garden has quickly prospered with financial support from various community groups. Volunteers have played an important role at the gardens from the very start and continue to lend support to programs and to help maintain the grounds.

HOURS

Daily, 9:00 a.m. to 5:00 p.m.

FEE

None

SIZE

85 acres along the Cape Fear River and Cross Creek

FEATURES

Woodland Rim Walk is a half-mile, well-kept trail winding through an oak forest. Native azaleas, atamasco lilies, and other native plants supply the garden with lots of color. There is also a natural amphitheater, picnic area, and Garden Pavilion.

DIRECTIONS

From I-95 take Exit 56 (Business 95/US 301). At 4.7 miles, cross the Cape Fear River. The garden will be on the left after crossing the river, directly across from the water-treatment facility.

TIPS

This garden is taking shape and growing, so don't mind the construction. Programs such as bird-watching and nature walks, gardening lectures, and evening classes related to gardening are offered. Some areas of the garden are handicapped accessible.

Bicentennial Garden

Greensboro Beautiful, Inc.
P.O. Box 3136
Greensboro, North Carolina 27402-3136
910-373-2558

HISTORY

*U*ndertaken in the early 1970s in anticipation of our country's bicentennial, this garden was completed and dedicated in 1976. The property, originally an overgrown part of the city's flood plain used for road fill, is adjacent to the David Caldwell Log College Historical Site. Since its beginning, the garden landscape has changed as new beds are planted and old ones renovated. In 1982, a hillside portion of the garden was planted in native azaleas and camellias to create a haven for birds and other suburban wildlife.

HOURS

Daily, sunrise to sunset

FEE

None

SIZE

7½ acres

FEATURES

Color saturates this garden in the springtime, as thousands of bulbs, azaleas, roses, and camellias burst into bloom. A stream, teeming with tiny creatures, intersects the garden, adding a dimension of sound which encourages the visitor to relax on one of the benches scattered throughout the garden. Other garden features include perennials, annuals, a fragrance and herb garden, and a rose-garden gazebo.

DIRECTIONS

From I-40 take Exit 214 (Wendover Avenue East). Turn right at the end of the ramp. At 3.6 miles, exit to Friendly Avenue. Turn left at the light and at 0.8 mile, turn right onto Hobbs Road. The garden entrance is to the left at 0.4 mile.

TIPS

This garden is at its peak in the spring when the bulbs, roses, and trees are blooming. All areas of the garden are handicapped accessible, as most of the paths are paved. Plan to visit the Bog Garden which is right across Hobbs Road. The Greensboro Arboretum is located two miles from this garden.

Benches at the Bicentennial Garden offer an invitation to the garden visitor to sit and enjoy the natural beauty of springtime.

The dense cover found at the Bog Garden provides the eastern cottontail rabbit with the perfect home.

GREENSBORO

Bog Garden

Greensboro Beautiful, Inc.
P.O. Box 3136
Greensboro, North Carolina 27402-3136
910-373-2558

HISTORY

The property that is now Greensboro's Bog Garden was donated to the city by Blanche Benjamin in 1987. Once the lake and surrounding property became part of the city, Dr. Joe Christian, a retired physician, began working to bring out the natural beauty of the water-soaked land. On first viewing the bog, Dr. Christian was met with weeds and debris; however, his vision went beyond the mess. He saw wildflowers peeking through weeds and lush green ferns camouflaging bits of trash. In his mind's eye, the bog began to take shape.

Volunteers rescued plants from developing properties around the area, transplanting them at the bog. In all, more than sixteen thousand plants have been added to the garden.

HOURS

Daily, sunrise to sunset

FEE

None

SIZE

21 acres, including a 4-acre lake

FEATURES

This small garden is a haven for native and migratory waterfowl. Home to countless trees, ferns, and wild roses, the garden can be seen from the raised boardwalk. The more agile and adventurous will enjoy the experience offered by a nature trail which features a three-hundred-year-old white oak and wildflowers galore.

DIRECTIONS

From I-40 take Exit 214 (Wendover Avenue East). Turn right at the end of the ramp. At 3.6 miles, exit to Friendly Avenue. Turn left at the light and at 0.8 mile turn right onto Hobbs Road. The garden entrance is to the right at 0.4 mile.

TIPS

Spring is the best time for the wildflowers. The water and cover offer the bird watcher the perfect place to observe our feathered friends. Most of the garden is accessible to the handicapped; but, trails may present some problems. The Bicentennial Garden is across Hobbs Road, and the Greensboro Arboretum is only two miles away.

Greensboro Arboretum

Greensboro Beautiful, Inc.
P.O. Box 3136
Greensboro, North Carolina 27402-3136
910-373-2558

HISTORY

*P*art of a tract of land donated to the city of Greensboro by J. Van Lindley in May 1918, the arboretum became a reality in 1986 when construction began. Completed in 1991, the arboretum, containing nine permanent plant collections, is located within a recreational area known as Lindley Park. Surrounded by several older neighborhoods, the arboretum was created through a collaborative effort between the parks and recreation department and Greensboro Beautiful, Inc. Their mission was to provide and promote a variety of educational opportunities for area students and a peaceful and enjoyable experience for visitors of all ages.

HOURS

Daily, sunrise to sunset

FEE

None

SIZE

17 acres

FEATURES

Paved and natural trails lace the arboretum's landscape. Weaving in and out of a woodland wonderland abundant with native and exotic wildflowers, the nature trails exercise the mind as well as the body. The arboretum features specific collections such as the Hydrophytic Garden, the Ground Cover Garden, the Butterfly Garden, the Winter Garden, the Small Tree Collection, the Rhododendron Garden, and many more displays.

DIRECTIONS

From I-40 take Exit 214 (Wendover Avenue East). Turn right at the end of the ramp. At 3.4 miles, exit to Market Street (US 421). At the end of the ramp, turn left and go under the bridge. Turn left at the next light, as if to return to Wendover Avenue. Once on the ramp to Wendover Avenue make an immediately right. Park in lots on either side of the baseball field. The arboretum is located behind the baseball field.

TIPS

Children will appreciate the arboretum's proximity to a well-equipped playground, while parents and other garden-goers will enjoy the diversity of the plantings. Approximately two miles of paved walkways allow broad access to the gardens for handicapped visitors. The arboretum is located within two miles of the Bog Garden and the Bicentennial Garden.

Black-eyed Susans line an embankment near one of the garden bridges at the Greensboro Arboretum.

Elizabethan Gardens

P.O. Box 1150
Manteo, North Carolina 27954-1150
919-473-3234

HISTORY

*A*merica's first English settlement vanished into
the New World wilderness in 1590, with only the word
"Croatoan," carved in a palisade of Fort Raleigh as a
clue. The mystery of their disappearance has never been
solved; but, the men and women of the settlement have
not been forgotten. In 1951, the Garden Club of North
Carolina created the Elizabethan Gardens as a living
memorial to the "Lost Colony." Designed by two renowned
United States landscape architects, M. Umberto Innocenti
and Richard Webel, the gardens are a true representa-
tion of an Elizabethan pleasure garden.

Protected on all sides by either a brick wall or by the
Roanoke Sound, the gardens are designed to offer color
at every season.

HOURS

Daily, 9:00 a.m. to 5:00 p.m.

FEE

Children under twelve are admitted free with a
paying adult. Discounts and special rates are available

SIZE

10 acres

FEATURES

These gardens, with their wide variety of native and
imported plants, are a delight for the professional and
amateur horticulturist alike. Typical English garden
structures add to the charm of the mixture of formal and
informal designs. There are several areas the garden visitor will find particularly appealing, such as the Queen's
Rose Garden, the Sunken Garden, the ancient live oak,
and the collections of camellias and rhododendron.

DIRECTIONS

The gardens are located on Roanoke Island just off US
64/264. Signs clearly mark the entrance. Gardens are
accessed by the park road into Fort Raleigh National
Historic Site.

TIPS

Designed as a pleasure garden, the landscape offers a
variety of blooming plants year round; however, the
spring flush of bloom is the most spectacular. The handicapped visitor may experience some difficulty as some
pathways are sandy. Guided tours of the gardens are
available by prearrangement.

The Sunken Garden, with its clipped hedges and symmetrical design, gives one the feel of England during colonial times.

Tryon Palace and Gardens

610 Pollock Street
New Bern, North Carolina 28560-5614
919-638-1560

HISTORY

Home to North Carolina's royal governor William Tryon and site of the state's first colonial capital, Tryon Palace seems very English and so do the gardens. Devastated by fire in 1798 and not rebuilt until 1952, the palace was restored using the original architectural renderings. The gardens, however, were reconstructed using design elements from both the eighteenth and nineteenth centuries, as no drawings were found which depicted the gardens as they would have appeared in 1798.

Formal design features popular in the eighteenth century work beautifully with the naturalized nineteenth-century style also employed in the gardens' design. The highly manicured features of the gardens dominate the palace landscape .

HOURS

Monday through Saturday
9:30 a.m. to 5:00 p.m.

Sunday
1:00 p.m. to 5:00 p.m.

FEE

Yes, some discounts are available

SIZE

14 acres, including gardens at the John Wright Stanly House and the George W. Dixon House

FEATURES

Combinations of eighteenth- and nineteenth-century design complement one another in this English-style garden. The most striking features are the "privy," or walled, gardens typical of Dutch and French gardens of the era. Other features of importance are the Maude Moore Latham Garden, the Green Garden, the Wilderness Area, the Kitchen Garden, and the modern Southern Garden. Seasonal displays of bulbs, annuals, and chrysanthemums add color throughout the year.

DIRECTIONS

Take US 17 into New Bern. It becomes Broad Street (US 17/70-NC 55). Cross Darst Avenue and turn right at the next street which is Bern Street. Signs will direct you to parking for the palace complex.

Tulips of Tryon Gardens provide a dramatic spring display.

A craft-shop window displays items reminiscent of the past.

The Walled Garden at Tryon Palace typifies eighteenth-century Dutch and French garden design.

TIPS

Spring at Tryon Palace is greeted each year by more than thirty-five thousand tulips, making it one of the most colorful times at the gardens. Most areas of the complex are accessible to the handicapped. Wheelchairs are available.

Sandhills Horticultural Gardens

2200 Airport Road
Pinehurst, North Carolina 28374-8299
910-695-3882 or 910-692-6185

HISTORY

On November 7, 1963, the Sandhills Community College was chartered. Five years later, the Landscape Gardening School was opened. Recognized nationally for its expertise in educational techniques and its highly qualified graduates, the Landscape Gardening School exists to further the training of students in the field of applied horticulture. The formal and informal gardens were designed, constructed, and planted by students to demonstrate the wide variety of plants available for the home landscape.

The college is supported in its efforts by the Sandhills Horticultural Society which offers public membership and private support to the garden. Throughout the year, the society sponsors garden-related activities and supplies docents and other volunteers to assist the college.

HOURS

Daily, sunrise to sunset

FEE

None

SIZE

23 acres

FEATURES

The Ebersole Holly Garden was the first garden established at the college. Other gardens dedicated to various plant species or environments soon followed, rounding out the collections. On the grounds are the Rose Garden, the Sir Walter Raleigh Garden, the Hillside Garden, the Fruit and Vegetable Garden, the Desmond Native Wetland Garden, and the Conifer Garden. Many gardens have decorative structures, fountains, or trellises. A boardwalk allows easy access to the Wetland Garden.

DIRECTIONS

At the Pinehurst traffic circle (the convergence of US 15/501, NC 2, and NC 211) take the NC 2 exit. After one hundred yards, turn left onto Airport Road. The college will be on the right at 2.3 miles. The gardens are located behind Heutte Hall.

TIPS

Group tours conducted by docents can be scheduled by calling the college. The garden is accessible to the handicapped visitor.

A covered trellis provides a shady resting spot with a view of the Fountain Courtyard in the Sir Walter Raleigh Garden.

Mordecai Historic Park

1 Mimosa Street
Raleigh, North Carolina 27610-1297
919-834-4844

HISTORY

*H*enry Lane, son of Joel Lane, the "Father of Raleigh," lived in the house his father built for him on land granted to the family by King George III. The city of Raleigh stands on what was once the bulk of the Lane plantation. In the early 1800s, Moses Mordecai married Henry's daughter, Margaret. After Margaret's death, Mordecai married her sister, Ann, thus adding the name of Mordecai to the Lane's house.

Mordecai, a lawyer, is credited with enlarging the house, once the core of the plantation, to its present size. Now, the plantation is home to history, and the kitchen garden feeds only the imagination. Recreated from Ellen Mordecai's book, *Gleanings From Long Ago*, the garden is planted as she described it during the early 1800s.

HOURS

Monday through Friday
10:00 a.m. to 3:00 p.m.
Saturday and Sunday
1:30 p.m. to 3:30 p.m.

Closed Holidays

FEE

Grounds are free, admission charged for buildings

SIZE

2¾ acres

FEATURES

The Mordecai House Kitchen Garden displays flowers, fruits, vegetables, and herbs typical of a nineteenth-century home garden.

DIRECTIONS

From I-40 take the I-440 Beltline (Exit 293). Exit I-440 at Wake Forest Road (Exit 10) and turn right. At 1.8 miles, exit Wake Forest Road to Downtown Boulevard. At 1.8 miles, turn left onto Jones Road. Travel 0.4 mile and turn left onto Person Street, stay in left lane. At 0.7 mile veer to left and cross Delway Street. Turn right onto Mimosa Street at 0.1 mile.

TIPS

A tour of the historic buildings is recommended to appreciate this small garden. Guided tours are offered and handicapped parking is available. Some buildings may present problems for individuals with limited mobility.

Benches offer all visitors to the Kitchen Garden at Mordecai Historic Park a place to rest.

N. C. State University Arboretum

Department of Horticultural Science
N.C. State University Box 7609
Raleigh, North Carolina 27695-7609
919-515-7641

HISTORY

Established in 1976 and dedicated in 1980, the N. C. State University Arboretum was the direct result of the need to enhance the horticultural programs in ornamental and landscape design offered by the university. A relatively young arboretum, the phenomenal growth it has experienced is due largely to the financial support it receives from individuals and corporations. The facility and grounds are planted and maintained by dedicated students and a group of active volunteers. Serving the students as an outdoor classroom and the community as a demonstration garden is the primary function of the arboretum; however, it is also an integral part of the research community. Growing and evaluating numerous species and cultivars of shrubs and trees, the arboretum is a testing ground for all types of plants destined for the North Carolina landscape.

HOURS

Daily, 8:00 a.m. to sunset

FEE

None

SIZE

8 acres

FEATURES

More than six thousand species of rare and unusual plants from forty-five countries are on display. Popular exhibits include the White Garden, reminiscent of the famous Sissinghurst Garden, the Magnolia Garden, the Shade House, the Rose Garden, the Japanese Garden, the Reading Garden, the Victorian Gazebo, and a three-hundred-foot perennial border. Other displays featured at the arboretum are collections of dwarf loblolly pine, red-bark Japanese crepe myrtle, and ground-cover junipers. Model landscapes appropriate for use by home gardeners are also on display.

Plentiful blooms supply a rainbow of colors along the three-hundred-foot perennial border.

DIRECTIONS

From I-40 take the I-440 Beltline (Exit 293). Exit I-440 at Hillsborought Street (Exit 3) and turn left at the end of the ramp. At 0.1 mile, turn right onto Beryl Road. The arboretum will be on the left at 0.5 mile.

TIPS

The perennial border is magnificent in either spring or fall. Tours conducted by area master gardeners are offered on Sundays at 2:00 p.m. from mid-April through mid-October. The garden is accessible to the handicapped.

Raleigh Municipal Rose Garden

Parks and Recreation Office
P. O. Box 590
Raleigh, North Carolina 27602-0590
919-890-3285   or   919-831-6059

HISTORY

*L*ocated on part of the former North Carolina Agricultural Fairgrounds, the Raleigh Municipal Rose Garden's existence is due in large part to Cantey Venable Sutton. Mrs. Sutton's father, Francis Venable, was president of the University of North Carolina, and her husband, Louis V. Sutton, was president of Carolina Power and Light. Her family had always been dedicated to public service, so it was no surprise when she took up the cause of a Works Progress Administration project to build a theater, amphitheater, and rose garden in Raleigh.

The buildings were completed in September 1940. However, landscaping was delayed by World War II, and it wasn't until March 1948 that the first roses were planted.

HOURS

Daily, sunrise to sunset

FEE

None

SIZE

6½ acres

FEATURES

This garden is planted with nearly twelve hundred roses. There is a pergola covered in Old Garden roses and sixty beds planted with hybrid tea, grandiflora, and floribunda roses. A fountain provides a focal point for the garden. Other features include a covered pavilion and an amphitheater. Seasonal annuals and bulbs are also displayed on the grounds.

DIRECTIONS

From I-40 take the I-440 Beltline (Exit 293). Exit I-440 at Hillsborough Street (Exit 3) and turn left. At 7.5 miles, turn left onto Pogue Street. The garden is located behind the Raleigh Little Theater at 301 Pogue Street.

TIPS

Mid-May through June is when the roses are at their peak. Parking is on Pogue Street. Grassy pathways may present some difficulty for the handicapped. Handicapped parking is behind the theater.

WRAL Azalea Gardens

2619 Western Boulevard
Raleigh, North Carolina 27606-2125
919-821-8555   or   919-879-1061

HISTORY

*M*r. A. J. Fletcher, chairman and chief executive officer of Capitol Broadcasting Company, was the force behind the WRAL Azalea Gardens until his death in 1979 at age 91. He assumed leadership of the Capitol Broadcasting Company in the mid-1950s, upon retiring from his law practice. His office at the television station had a glass exterior wall overlooking an expansive lawn. Fletcher decided the lawn needed some color, so he set about planning a garden. He wanted to be able to sit at his desk and see colorful blooms spread out before him.

The question of what to plant on the lawn was solved when Fletcher discovered that a nursery in South Carolina was disposing of its azalea stock. He bought the entire stock and had it shipped to Raleigh. The plants were divided between the WRAL property and Montlawn Memorial Park, a cemetery Fletcher founded with North Carolina Governor Melville Broughton. The gardens were only one of the many projects initiated by A. J. Fletcher. He also founded the Capitol Broadcasting Company and the National Opera Company.

HOURS

Daily, sunrise to sunset

FEE

None

SIZE

5 acres

FEATURES

Two thousand azaleas make the gardens a springtime spectacle. Pathways wind their way through mature azalea plantings, which open onto small clearings where benches and other surprises await. The gardens also feature a variety of flowering trees and perennials.

DIRECTIONS

From I-40 take the I-440 Beltline (Exit 293). Exit I-440 at Western Boulevard (Exit 2A). At 1.5 miles, the gardens will be on the right.

TIPS

This is a popular place for weddings, so you may want to avoid certain parts of the gardens during services. Parking may also be a problem while weddings are in progress. Portions of the gardens are handicapped accessible.

Flora Macdonald Gardens

P.O. Box 547
Red Springs, North Carolina 28377-0547
910-843-5000

HISTORY

*I*n 1896, Reverend Charles Graves Vardell founded a school for young ladies in the Cape Fear region of North Carolina. The reverend preached "that the most desirable thing in the world was a cultured Christian woman." In no time, he amassed enough donations to erect the first building of the Southern Presbyterian College and Conservatory of Music. In May 1914, the Scottish Society of America petitioned to have the name of the school changed to the Flora Macdonald College in honor of the heroine of Skye, Scotland, and savior of Charles Stuart, the last crowned king of Scotland.

The grounds around the newly built college were swampy and in need of improvement, so Reverend Vardell and his assistant, Dexter Garner, set to work. For forty years, they worked diligently to transform the tiny campus into an informal botanical garden. Some of the gardens were reclaimed by the swamp after a tornado devastated the grounds in 1984; however, progress has been made in bringing the gardens back to their original state of beauty.

HOURS

Daily, 9:00 a.m. to 5:00 p.m.
October 1 through March 31
Daily, 9:00 a.m. to 7:00 p.m.
April 1 through September 30

FEE

None

SIZE

13 acres along Little Raft Swamp

FEATURES

Etched out of the Little Raft Swamp, the gardens are known for their azaleas. Other features include camellias, a small planting of roses, a boardwalk, and a tree-lined allée.

DIRECTIONS

From I-95 take NC 211 North (Exit 20) to Red Springs. NC 211 becomes Main Street. Turn right onto Third Street. At 0.2 mile, turn left onto College Street, and at 0.1 mile, the gardens are on the right.

TIPS

During rainy periods the gardens can become soggy. Grassy pathways and a boardwalk with steps could present problems for the handicapped.

Chinqua-Penn Plantation

2138 Wentworth Street
Reidsville, North Carolina 27320-7304
910-349-4576

HISTORY

*T*homas Jefferson "Jeff" Penn believed, "Places as well as people must have an appealing personality if they would carry on to some permanent influence . . ." To that end, he and his wife, Betsy, worked to create the uniquely beautiful Chinqua-Penn Plantation. The name, a play on words, refers to the chinquapin tree, a dwarf member of the chestnut family, and to the Penns. The couple lived in the mansion until their deaths, his in January 1946, and hers in February 1965.

In 1959, Betsy Penn turned ownership of the plantation over to the University of North Carolina system on the condition she would retain the estate for the rest of her life. In 1966, the year after her death, Chinqua-Penn was opened as a museum. Its doors closed for a short time in 1986 due to a lack of funding, but reopened under the auspices of N. C. State University. Citing financial difficulties, the plantation closed again in 1991, but re-opened in July 1994 under the guidance of the Chinqua-Penn Foundation, Inc..

HOURS

Tuesday through Saturday
10:00 a.m. to 6:00 p.m.
Sunday
1:00 p.m. to 6:00 p.m.
Closed
January and February,
July 4th, Thanksgiving, and Christmas Day

FEE

Yes, tickets only for the grounds are available

SIZE

22 acres

FEATURES

Many native plants and exotic species are on display. Of particular interest are the Chinese Pagoda Gardens, the Goldfish Pools, the Herb Gardens, the Rose Garden, and the Formal Garden.

DIRECTIONS

From I-85 or I-40, take US 29 North to NC 14 North. At 3.5 miles, turn left onto Salem Church Road. At Wentworth Street turn right and go 0.3 mile.

TIPS

Chinqua-Penn Plantation puts on a Christmas display beginning in early December. The plantation is accessible to the handicapped visitor.

Elizabeth Holmes Hurley Park

P. O. Box 479
Salisbury, North Carolina 28145-0479
704-638-5260   or   704-638-5255

HISTORY

*N*amed in memory of Mrs. Elizabeth Holmes Hurley, one of Salisbury's first residents in the City Lake area, this park is a fine example of what cooperation can bring to a community. Mrs. Hurley died in 1984. That same year, the city of Salisbury and the J. F. Hurley (Mrs. Hurley's husband) Foundation began working together to develop a master plan for a park in the City Lake neighborhood. The master plan was created by the Sears Design Group of Raleigh, North Carolina, and implemented cooperatively by the city and the J. F. Hurley Foundation to provide a haven for wildlife and a memorable experience for visitors.

HOURS

Daily, sunrise to sunset

FEE

None

SIZE

15 acres

FEATURES

Year-round beauty is offered by this quiet park. Whether it's spring wildflowers or bright red holly berries in wintertime, the colors and textures of this garden will surprise and delight you. Other features include magnolias, azaleas, and perennials. The visitor can enjoy woodland trails, gazebos, bridges, and benches located throughout the park. All plants are clearly labeled to assist gardeners with plant identification.

DIRECTIONS

From I-85 take Exit 76B. Turn right at the end of the ramp onto West Innis Street. At 2.3 miles, turn right onto Mahaley Avenue. Mahaley Avenue becomes Confederate Avenue after crossing Mocksville Avenue. Continue for 3.5 miles to Lake Drive. Turn right onto Lake Drive and the park is on the right.

TIPS

Paved pathways provide handicapped access to almost the entire park. Some areas, such as the woodland trail and bridges, may present problems for the handicapped.

The winding paths and footbridges at Elizabeth Holmes Hurley Park are framed by the decorative arch of a gazebo.

Wilkes Community College Gardens

P.O. Box 120
Wilkesboro, North Carolina 28697-0120
910-651-8600

HISTORY

*T*n September 1964, the voters of Wilkes County decided to fund a community college. Over the years, the college has become an integral part of the Wilkesboro community. The Wilkes Community College Visitor Center is considered to be the hub of tourism in the county. The center also serves as the gateway to the Wilkes Community College Gardens, which began informally with the planting of a single Japanese maple tree.

In 1985, the trustees of the college acted upon a recommendation by F. W. Townes, dean of development, to formally develop the gardens at the college. Community support of the gardens has made them a success. The gardens' most famous benefactor is Grammy award-winning bluegrass artist, "Doc" Watson. In April, Merle Fest, a bluegrass festival, is held in memory of Doc's son, Eddy Merle Watson. Merle Fest benefits the Eddy Merle Watson Memorial Garden for the Senses.

HOURS

Daily, sunrise to midnight

FEE

None

SIZE

30 garden areas on 130 acres of campus

FEATURES

There are gardens galore on this campus, with the Eddy Merle Watson Memorial Garden for the Senses being the most elaborate. The main feature of this garden is the seventy-foot wall titled *Nature's Alphabet and the Tree of Memories*. Carved from concrete and brick by Goldsboro artist Patricia Turlington, the wall encourages the visually impaired to touch and experience texture and form. Other features include the Vernon and Louise Deal Native Garden, the Ron Stanley Victory Vegetable Garden, the Sara Mills Japanese Garden, the Whitley Log Cabin, a woodland trail, and a wildflower meadow. There is a well-equipped playground for children.

The Tree of Memories, *sculpted by Patricia Turlington, in the Eddy Merle Watson Memorial Garden for the Senses.*

DIRECTIONS

From I-40 take Exit 188 (US 421 North). In Wilkesboro at the junction of US 421 and NC 268, take the Wilkes Community College exit. Turn left at the end of the ramp. At 0.3 mile, turn left onto Collegiate Road. The Wilkes Community College Visitor Center and Gardens parking lot will be on the left at 0.5 mile.

TIPS

Start your tour of the gardens at the visitor center. Maps and brochures will make your visit more enjoyable. Handicapped parking is available and great care has been taken to make the garden as accessible as possible to senior citizens and the handicapped. Call or write the college for additional information on Merle Fest.

Airlie Gardens

P. O. Box 210
Wilmington, North Carolina 28402-0210
910-763-4646

HISTORY

*A*irlie Gardens is a privately owned coastal garden paradise originally owned by wealthy New York financier Pembroke Jones and his wife, Sarah. The property was named Airlie after Pembroke Jones's ancestral home in Scotland. Jones purchased the property from the Wright family so Sarah could retreat to a sequestered "cabin" in the woods. The original structure at Airlie was a simple, two-room dwelling; however, this was soon replaced with a thirty-five-room mansion capable of accommodating eighty guests.

Pembroke and Sarah made the permanent move to Airlie in 1895 when their home, now known as the Governor Dudley Mansion, in Wilmington proper caught fire. Airlie now belongs to the descendants of Wilmington industrialist W. Albert Corbett and has been opened to the public. The Pembroke Jones mansion at Airlie is no longer standing; however, the gardens are still magnificent. Located along Bradley Creek and the Wrightsville Sound, the gardens overlook infamous Money Island. The island is supposed to be the final resting place for buried treasure amassed by the notorious pirate, Captain Kidd.

HOURS

Daily, 8:00 a.m. to 5:00 p.m.
March through April
Daily, 9:00 a.m. to 5:00 p.m.
May 1 through September

FEE

Yes

SIZE

155 acres along Bradley Creek

FEATURES

Azaleas and camellias provide an abundance of real and reflected color along the banks of a garden lake. Magnificent live oaks, ancient and covered with moss, are surrounded by even more azaleas and camellias. Graceful swans add a formal touch to the otherwise informal garden landscape. Other features at the gardens are the Spring Garden (the only formal garden at Airlie), a stone pergola, and an old rural Episcopal chapel, Lebanon Chapel, built in 1825. There is a picnic area and restroom facilities near the chapel.

Swans add a touch of elegance to the otherwise informal landscape of Airlie Gardens.

DIRECTIONS

I-40 East becomes North College Road just north of Wilmington. Stay on North College Road until the junction with US 76 (Oleander Drive). Turn left onto Oleander (east) and at 3.5 miles cross the Bradley Creek bridge. Airlie Road will be on your right at 0.3 mile.

TIPS

Visit the gardens in early April and take time to enjoy the North Carolina Azalea Festival held in Wilmington. The gardens may be toured either by car or on foot. Handicapped individuals can view most of the gardens from a vehicle.

Greenfield Gardens

City of Wilmington
P. O. Box 1810
Wilmington, North Carolina 28402-1810
910-341-7852   or   910-341-7855

HISTORY

Greenfield Gardens, Wilmington's municipal lake and recreation center, is one of North Carolina's finest civic gardens. It is located on part of a plantation formerly owned by Dr. Samuel Green. Dr. Green, physician and native of Liverpool, England, lived on the plantation with his family and second wife Hannah until his death in 1771. The property was left to Hannah and was eventually sold by Dr. Green's children to T.C. McIlhenny.

In 1857, the McIlhenny family advertised the sale of the property. Privately owned and used as a carnival site until the city of Wilmington purchased the property in 1925, Greenfield Gardens became a community improvement project which lasted through the depression years. Work at the gardens provided jobs for more than fifteen hundred Wilmington residents during the Great Depression.

HOURS

Daily, 7:00 a.m. to 11:00 p.m.

FEE

None

SIZE

150 acres, including a 130-acre lake

FEATURES

The five-mile scenic drive and the millions of azaleas are Greenfield Gardens' claim to fame. Dogwoods, magnolias, crepe myrtles, camellias, and roses all add to the variety of plants and colors experienced throughout the growing season. Cypress trees stand proud in the black water of Greenfield Lake, and live oak trees line the shore. Other features include seasonal canoe and paddleboat rentals, tennis courts, a fragrance garden, a nature trail, a multi-purpose trail, an amphitheater, and picnic areas.

DIRECTIONS

I-40 East becomes North College Road just north of Wilmington. At Market Street (US 17/74), exit North College Road and turn left onto Market Street. At 4.5 miles, turn left onto Third Street. At 1 mile, Third Street becomes Burnett Boulevard. The gardens are on the left side of Burnett Boulevard.

The glow of the setting sun shines on a stand of bald cypress trees draped with Spanish moss.

Dark waters of Greenfield Lake reflect bald cypress trees just before dawn.

Lion's Bridge crosses Square Branch, where dogwoods and azaleas decorate the banks.

TIPS

Start your visit by touring the lake on the five-mile scenic drive beginning at the park office. Children will enjoy the play areas and the water-related activities available during warmer months. Some areas of the park are handicapped accessible.

A tiny island in the goldfish pool is accessed by a footbridge at the New Hanover County Extension Service Arboretum.

New Hanover County Extension Service Arboretum

6202 Oleander Drive
Wilmington, North Carolina 28403-3534
910-452-6393

HISTORY

*T*he development of the New Hanover County Extension Service Arboretum began in the early 1980s as a way for the county extension service to broaden its ornamental horticulture programs. The site eventually selected for the arboretum was once a school playground and included two buildings remaining from a fire. Easy public access, mature live oak trees, and other native flora made this property suitable for the new arboretum.

Community and volunteer support have been invaluable in helping the arboretum, the only one in southeastern North Carolina, reach its goal of creating a place where gardeners with varying levels of expertise can study plants and their environment.

HOURS

Daily, sunrise to sunset

FEE

None

SIZE

6½ acres

FEATURES

The arboretum has several thousand plants specifically suited to coastal conditions. There are thirty-two different plant collections, including an aquatic garden, a rose garden, a shade garden, and a perennial garden. A conservatory displays a miniature rain forest and exotic plants from all over the world.

DIRECTIONS

I-40 East becomes North College Road just north of Wilmington. Stay on North College Road until the junction with US 76 (Oleander Drive). Turn left onto Oleander Drive, the garden is on the right at 3 miles.

TIPS

This is a gardener's garden. A true kaleidoscope of natural colors make this arboretum a joy to visit from spring to the first pangs of winter. Handicapped parking, paved pathways, and ramps make the arboretum readily accessible to the handicapped.

Orton Plantation Gardens

RFD 1
Winnabow, North Carolina 28479-9701
910-371-6851

HISTORY

Orton Plantation, named for the English ancestral home of its first owner, Roger Moore, predates the gardens by at least 185 years. The gardens were started by James and Luola Sprunt in 1910. The Sprunts constructed terraces and planted camellias, azaleas, rhododendron, and other shrubs. Their son, James Lawrence Sprunt, enlarged the gardens to their current size and added a wide variety of ornamentals.

Once a thriving colonial rice plantation noted for the superior quality of its grain, Orton abandoned its rice farming after the nineteenth century. However, each winter the old rice fields are still flooded to provide food and shelter for migrating waterfowl and a variety of native animal and bird species.

HOURS

Daily, 8:00 a.m. to 6:00 p.m.
Spring and Summer

Daily, 8:00 a.m. to 5:00 p.m.
Autumn
Closed December 1 through February 2

FEE

Yes

SIZE

20 acres

FEATURES

The rice fields and ancient live oak trees of Orton Plantation Gardens offer a glimpse into the past. Each April the azaleas, camellias, and other ornamentals begin to bloom. The well-maintained gardens feature Luola's Chapel, the Radial Garden, the Scroll Garden, the Lagoon and the Chinese bridges, the Triangle Garden, and the Sun Garden.

DIRECTIONS

Orton is located 18 miles south of Wilmington off NC 133. Signs will direct you to the gardens.

TIPS

The gardens take approximately forty-five minutes to an hour to tour. The house is the private residence of the plantation owners and is not open to the public. Handicapped parking and wheelchairs are available.

The house at Orton Plantation Gardens is a perfect example of an antebellum mansion.

Plantings in the Scroll Garden paint
living pictures in the lush green grass.

Ancient live oaks gracefully shelter brick
pathways and spring-blooming azaleas.

Nodding sunflowers, planted in the communal garden, peer over an old, weather-worn picket fence at Bethabara Park.

Bethabara Park

2147 Bethabara Road
Winston-Salem, North Carolina   27106-2701
910-924-8191

HISTORY

*I*n 1753, a small group of Pennsylvania Moravians settled in the Carolina back country at a spot on the Great Wagon Road between Pennsylvania and Georgia. They called their new home Bethabara, which means "House of Passage," and the tiny settlement became the first Moravian settlement in North Carolina. Here, the German-speaking Moravians built their *Gemeinhaus* (church with attached living quarters) and worked their communal garden. This garden is the only known, well-documented colonial community garden in the United States. Today, local gardeners carry on the community-garden tradition by planting varieties thought to have been grown by the first settlers.

HOURS

Grounds
All day, year round
Buildings
Monday through Friday
9:30 a.m. to 4:30 p.m.
Saturday and Sunday

1:30 p.m. to 4:30 p.m.
April 1 through November 30

FEE

None

SIZE

110 acres

FEATURES

Communal living was an economic fact of life in old Bethabara, and the one-acre community garden is a vivid reminder of this bygone necessity. The park has more than six miles of nature trails and is rich in history. The museum features restored buildings, a 1788 Moravian church, archaeological ruins, and a visitor center.

DIRECTIONS

From I-40 Business take the Cherry Street Exit. Cherry Street is one way. At 2.5 miles, Cherry Street becomes University Parkway. Go another 1.5 miles to Bethabara Road. Turn left and go 1.2 miles to the park.

TIPS

Bethabara Park is an excellent trip for the gardener who happens to be a history buff. The visitor center is handicapped accessible.

Old Salem Gardens

P.O. Box F
Winston-Salem, North Carolina 27108-0346
800-441-5305 or 910-721-7300

HISTORY

*I*n 1766, the Moravians moved their town of Bethabara a little south and renamed it Salem, from the Hebrew word *shalom* meaning "peace." The town prospered, as did the neighboring community of Winston, founded in 1849. However, Winston's growth, due to the textile and tobacco industries, overshadowed the cottage industry embraced by Salem residents. So, in 1913, the two towns consolidated to become Winston-Salem. Today, many of the original buildings of Salem still survive and have been painstakingly restored. Other building have been faithfully reconstructed on their original sites. The old "town," now known as Old Salem, has been landscaped to recreate the feel of the eighteenth century. Period street lamps, costumed guides, and craftsmen help add to the historical flavor of Old Salem.

HOURS

Monday through Saturday
9:30 a.m. to 4:30 p.m.

Sunday
1:30 p.m. to 4:30 p.m.
Exhibit buildings and gift shops are closed
Thanksgiving Day, Christmas Eve, and Christmas Day

FEE

Grounds are free. Admission is charged for touring the houses and community buildings. Combination tickets may be purchased and certain discounts are available.

SIZE

11 period family gardens, 5½ acres of orchards, 24 blocks of shops, houses, and public buildings

FEATURES

Medicinal gardens, kitchen gardens, and cutting gardens are tucked away behind worn picket fences and beside restored homes. Plants on display are believed to have been grown during the days when Salem was a thriving community. Today the gardens add charm and color to the landscape while beckoning the visitor to linger awhile in the quiet past. Other features in Old

Family gardens throughout Old Salem are planted in the style popular during the eighteenth century.

Salem include the commons in the center of town and ninety restored buildings, of which twelve are open to the public. There are communal buildings, the Sisters House and the Single Brothers House, and shops such as Shultz's Shoemaker Shop, Winkler Bakery, and Miksch Tobacco Shop, which depict crafts from the eighteenth century. Many more historical buildings provide a glimpse into the past. All tours begin at the visitor center located at 600 South Main Street.

DIRECTIONS

Old Salem is located near downtown. Follow the brown historical markers from I-40, I-40 Business, and US 52.

TIPS

Old Salem covers twenty-four blocks so wear comfortable shoes. There is a restaurant adjacent to the visitor center and handicapped parking is available.

Early morning mist settles on the garden entrance of the conservatory and greenhouses at Reynolda Gardens.

Reynolda Gardens of Wake Forest University

100 Reynolda Village
Winston-Salem, North Carolina 27106-5123
910-759-5593

HISTORY

Reynolda Gardens are named for Richard Joshua Reynolds, the original owner of the estate and founder of the R. J. Reynolds Tobacco Company. In 1914, while his country home was under construction, Reynolds and his wife, Katharine, decided that they wanted the surrounding gardens to reflect the relaxed country lifestyle they hoped to enjoy. In 1916, they engaged Thomas W. Sears of Philadelphia to create a country paradise. Sears used 130 acres of the estate's original 1,067 acres to create a mix of formal and informal gardens, woodland trails, and expansive lawns.

In 1934, Mary Reynolds Babcock, daughter of Katharine and R. J. Reynolds, and her husband, Charles, renovated the family house and added recreational facilities. The gardens, greenhouses, and conservatory were donated to Wake Forest University in 1958. In 1964, the Babcocks donated the house as a museum.

HOURS

Grounds
Daily, sunrise to sunset
Conservatory and greenhouses
Monday through Saturday
10:00 a.m. to 4:00 p.m.

FEE

None

SIZE

130-acre estate, including 4 acres of formal gardens

FEATURES

Flagstone pathways, leading in and around planting areas, are lined with American boxwoods and dotted with flowering crab apple trees. The crab apples are underplanted with different flowering plants during the growing season. Tulips bloom in the spring, followed by impatiens and other seasonal annuals. Trees provide ample shade over many of the benches located throughout the gardens. Four acres of the grounds are devoted to the formal garden arrangement, emphasizing plants available for the home garden. The gardener may imitate

Rows of terra cotta pots await the next planting season.

A light dusting of flowering crab apple petals cover the boxwoods and tulips like newly fallen snow.

any part of the Perennial Garden, the Home Vegetable Garden, or the Herb Garden. Suggestions for roses suited to the Piedmont can be determined by browsing through the All-American Rose Selections Garden. If the less-formal garden atmosphere is more to your liking, woodland trails, winding through pine trees and hardwoods, offer an extravaganza of color when native dogwoods and wildflowers bloom. Exotic plants, which may pique your interest, can be found in the greenhouses. The conservatory houses a collection of tropical plants.

In the early spring, daffodils brighten the nature trails beneath the woodland canopy.

DIRECTIONS

From I-40 East Business take the Cherry Street Exit (one way). At 2.3 miles, turn left onto Coliseum Drive. At 1.2 miles, turn right onto Reynolda Road. Entrance to the gardens will be on the right at Reynolda Village. From I-40 West Business take the Wake Forest University/Silas Creek Parkway Exit. At 4.2 miles, turn right onto Reynolda Road. The entrance to the gardens will be on the left at Reynolda Village.

TIPS

These lovely gardens deserve your attention on any spring day; however, visitors will find a wide array of blooming plants throughout the growing season. A thorough understanding of the lifestyle of the Reynolds family can be obtained by visiting the house in conjunction with the gardens. Narrow pathways and steps may present problems for the handicapped. Parking for the handicapped is available.

The American Pillar rose is one of many trellis-trained roses in the rose garden located near the Doll House.

Colorful plantings that change with the seasons surround the pergola, lily pond, and fountain.

South Carolina

The Live Oak Allée at Brookgreen Gardens in Murrells Inlet

Hopeland Gardens and Rye Patch

P. O. Box 1107
Aiken South Carolina 29802-1107
803-642-7630

HISTORY

*H*opeland Gardens and Rye Patch were once adjoining estates used as winter residences by their wealthy owners. Hopeland Gardens was named for Hope Goddard Iselin, the wife of Oliver Iselin. Rye Patch was the home of Dorothy Knox Goodyear Rogers and her husband, Edmund. Both women were keenly interested in horses, Mrs. Iselin in racing and Mrs. Rogers in riding. They also shared a common interest in developing the gardens on their respective properties.

In order to preserve her gardens at Hopeland for others to enjoy, Mrs. Iselin willed the property to the city of Aiken upon her death, at age 102, in 1970. The Iselin home was razed as it would have been costly to repair; but, the stable is now a museum. Rye Patch Estate was given to the city by the children of Mrs. Rogers after her death in 1980. The house, guest cottage, stables, and carriage house are still used by the city.

HOURS

Daily, 10:00 a.m. to sunset

FEE

Grounds are free. Admission is charged to visit Rye Patch House

SIZE

24 acres

FEATURES

Beautifully situated beneath ancient live oaks, the Hopeland Gardens and Rye Patch offer a myriad of plants to please every visitor. Crepe myrtle blooms soften the summer heat, and the fragrance from roses in the Memorial Rose Garden fill the spring air. Other plants, such as camellias, azaleas, magnolias, and dogwoods round out the long South Carolina growing season. The gardens also feature fountains, an amphitheater, statuary, and a Touch and Scent Trail for the visually impaired.

A second-story window at Hopeland stables, now the Thoroughbred Racing Hall of Fame, overlooks the gardens.

DIRECTIONS

From I-20 take Exit 22 (US 1). This becomes York Street. Follow York Street to its end at South Boundary Avenue. Turn right onto South Boundary Avenue and take the next left at Whiskey Road. At 0.2 mile, turn right onto Dupree Place. Gardens are at the corner of Dupree Place and Whiskey Road.

TIPS

Be sure to visit the Thoroughbred Racing Hall of Fame located within the park in a restored carriage house. Each April, nearby Augusta, Georgia, plays host to the Masters Golf Tournament which makes finding lodging difficult, so plan ahead. Some areas of the park may present problems for the handicapped.

Boone Hall Plantation

P. O. Box 1554
Mt. Pleasant, South Carolina 29465-1554
803-884-4371

HISTORY

*M*ajor John Boone, for whom Boone Hall was named, was among the first fleet of settlers to arrive in Charles Town in the late 1600s. In 1681, he received a land grant of seventeen thousand acres from the Lords Proprietor in England during the reign of King Charles II. In the eighteenth and nineteenth centuries, Boone Hall prospered as a cotton plantation; however, through the years, it became known for its brick and tile works. Bricks, handmade at Boone Hall Plantation, were used in the construction of many of the historic homes in Charleston, as well as in constructing the slave cabins of Boone Hall. Today nine of the original slave cabins built around 1743 still survive and are on the National Register of Historic Places. It is believed the live oak trees for the "Avenue of Oaks" were planted by Captain Thomas Boone at the same time the slave cabins were built.

HOURS

Monday through Saturday
8:30 a.m. to 6:30 p.m.

Sunday
1:00 p.m. to 5:00 p.m.
April 1 through Labor Day
Monday through Saturday
9:00 a.m. to 5:00 p.m.
Sunday
1:00 p.m. to 4:00 p.m.
The rest of the year
Closed Thanksgiving and Christmas

FEE

Yes, some discounts may apply

SIZE

738 acres

FEATURES

The most striking feature of Boone Hall Plantation is the half-mile "Avenue of Oaks," which stretches in front of the plantation house. Dripping with Spanish moss, the oaks are awe-inspiring at any time of the year; however, the plantation offers other horticultural delights. Formal gardens of azaleas and camellias planted in front of the restored mansion are laced with brick pathways. In the spring, tulips provide splashes of color which add to the beauty of the grounds.

Two-hundred-fifty-year-old live oak trees, planted by the original owner's son, line the half-mile drive to Boone Hall.

DIRECTIONS

From I-26 take Exit 212C (I-526 East) towards Mt. Pleasant. At 9.5 miles, take the Long Point Road Exit and turn left at the end of the ramp. The plantation and gardens will be on the left at 2.2 miles.

TIPS

History pervades the plantation and a tour of the house is recommended. The restored cotton gin houses a gift shop and a restaurant. The plantation and gardens are not handicapped accessible.

Drayton Hall

3380 Ashley River Road
Charleston, South Carolina   29414-7126
803-766-0188

HISTORY

When John Drayton left home to begin life on his own, he didn't travel far—just a few miles down river from his father's home, Magnolia Plantation. In 1742, John's home, Drayton Hall, was completed. Located on the Ashley River near Charleston, the stately plantation house of Georgian Palladian design is one of a few great southern houses surviving today. Standing steadfast against wars, natural disasters, vandals, and time, Drayton Hall is a magnificent reminder of the glory days of the southern colonial lifestyle enjoyed by the planter "aristocracy." Acquired by the National·Trust for Historic Preservation from the Drayton family in 1974, Drayton Hall is considered to be a "preserved" national treasure because the family, which used the house seasonally until 1969, resisted the urge to modernize. The Draytons, recognized as one of the wealthiest families in South Carolina, could have added whatever comforts suited them. Instead, they chose to preserve the family's ancestral home in its original state. The interior has been painted twice, once when it was built and again in 1875.

HOURS

Daily, 10:00 a.m. to 4:00 p.m.
March through October
Daily, 10:00 a.m. to 3:00 p.m.
November through February
Closed Thanksgiving, Christmas,
and New Year's Day

FEE

Yes

SIZE

650 acres on the Ashley River

FEATURES

Two-hundred-year-old oak trees are the primary attraction in this plantation-style garden. Azalea and camellia plantings, between the house and the Ashley River, add color in the spring and fall. Without a doubt, the house is the real standout at Drayton Hall Plantation. A pictorial record of the plantation, comprised of newspaper articles and photographs, is on hand at the museum shop. Guided tours are conducted in English, with written tours available in French and German.

Drayton Hall, built in 1742, is the only plantation home on the Ashley River that survived the Civil War.

DIRECTIONS

From I-26 take Exit 216A (SC 7 South) and follow the historic plantation signs on Rittenburg Boulevard. Turn right onto SC 61 North (Ashley River Road); the plantation will be on the right at 8 miles.

TIPS

Allow approximately forty-five minutes to an hour for the tour of the house and grounds. It is recommended that large groups and handicapped persons call in advance of their visit.

Hampton Park

Charleston Department of Parks & Recreation
30 Mary Murray Drive
Charleston, South Carolina 29403-4194
803-724-7321

HISTORY

The site of present-day Hampton Park was once John Gibbes' Orange Grove Plantation. In 1791, the plantation became the village of Washington. The Charleston Jockey Club purchased a fifty-five-acre tract and promptly established the Washington Race Course. When the club went out of business in 1900, the property was acquired by the Charleston Library Society. The tract owned by the library society, and another two hundred acres, were used by the city of Charleston to establish the grounds of the 1902 Carolina Interstate and West Indian Exposition. Designed to attract business to South Carolina, the exposition grounds were beautifully developed and well-furnished with exhibits that attracted international attention. When the exposition ended in May of 1902, the buildings and most of the grounds were razed. Only a small part of the landscaped Sunken Gardens remained. Those gardens are now the lagoon and rose walk area of Hampton Park. The park is named in honor of General Wade Hampton for his services to South Carolina. When the city received ownership of the park after the exposition, a great deal of work was needed to turn the bare acreage into a municipal park. In 1905, the Olmsted brothers of Boston were hired to develop a master plan for the 130-acre park. The plan was never completed because in 1918 almost half of the property was deeded to the state for construction of The Citadel, South Carolina's military academy.

HOURS

Daily, sunrise to sunset

FEE

None

SIZE

65 acres

FEATURES

In addition to the ancient oaks, the park offers a formal rose walk with over one hundred varieties of roses and plantings of azaleas, camellias, crepe myrtles, magnolias, and numerous perennials. There is an abundance of color from early spring through late fall. Walking paths, a fitness trail, an outdoor cafe, and picnic tables make outdoor recreation enjoyable. Also featured at the park is a restored Victorian bandstand and a fountain with a large lagoon that attracts numerous waterfowl.

The Sunken Gardens from the 1902 Carolina Interstate and West Indian Exposition are now a part of Hampton Park.

DIRECTIONS

From I-26 take Rutledge Avenue (Exit 219) and follow the signs to The Citadel. At 1 mile, turn right onto Cleveland Street just past the Riverdogs stadium.

TIPS

Concerts are held at the fountain during summer months. The Piccolo Spoleto finale is held in June. Most areas of the park are handicapped accessible.

Magnolia Plantation and Gardens

Route 4, Ashley River Road
Charleston, South Carolina 29414-7700
803-571-1266

HISTORY

*M*agnolia Plantation and Gardens are firmly rooted in the beginnings of South Carolina. Still owned by the Drayton family, who built the first plantation house of note in the colonies in the 1680s, Magnolia is home to the oldest major garden in the United States. Opened to the public more than one hundred years ago, the gardens were part of the original plan for the plantation, not added as an afterthought. The gardens were designed in the seventeenth-century English style and initially covered only ten acres. As time passed, the gardens slowly grew and changed with each Drayton heir.

It wasn't until the mid-1800s that the gardens began to take on a new significance. Reverend John Grimke Drayton wanted his wife, Julia, to forget her family home and come to love Magnolia Plantation as much as he did. To that end, he devoted himself to the gardens "to create an earthly paradise in which (his) dear Julia

(would) forever forget Philadelphia and her desire to return there." The reverend's plans for the earthly paradise were cut short by the Civil War, which left him in virtual poverty. Other Drayton descendants sought to improve the property and, like the good reverend, were sidetracked by events beyond their control. The crash of 1929 thwarted the rebuilding of a mansion similar to the original. In 1975, the existing house was turned into a museum and opened to the public. The family still owns the plantation.

HOURS

Daily, 8:00 a.m. to 5:00 p.m.

FEE

Yes, some discounts apply and combination tickets are available

SIZE

500 acres on the Ashley River

Black swamp water, dotted with fallen dogwood petals, moves slowly beneath the footbridge and a bald cypress tree.

The Canada goose is one species of waterfowl which calls Magnolia Plantation home.

A live oak tree is surrounded by bountiful spring blooms of native azaleas. Statues of various design dot the gardenscape.

FEATURES

The gardens at Magnolia Plantation are filled with wondrous delights for all members of the family. The fifty acres of landscaped gardens are famous for their spring displays of azaleas and the winter flourish of more than nine hundred varieties of camellias. Another spectacular feature at the plantation is the Barbados Tropical Garden, a seven-thousand-square-foot solarium teeming with plants indigenous to Barbados. There are other attractions, such as the 125-acre Waterfowl Refuge, the Wildlife Observation Tower, nature and bike trails, the Herb and Biblical gardens, the Maze, and the Topiary Gardens. Animals are also part of the charm at Magnolia, especially the rare miniature horses. The Audubon Swamp Garden, a separate attraction, is a sixty-acre, black-water-swamp home to many species of wildlife.

Eighteenth-century design is employed in several areas of the garden.

Sheep graze in pasture surrounded by ancient live oak trees.

DIRECTIONS

From I-26 take Exit 216A (SC 7 South) and follow the historic plantation signs on Rittenburg Boulevard. Turn right onto SC 61 North (Ashley River Road). The plantation and gardens will be on the right at 10 miles. Magnolia Plantation is located between Drayton Hall and Middleton Place.

TIPS

With so much to see, it is important to begin your visit to Magnolia Plantation and Gardens as soon as it opens. Plan to spend at least three hours; however, realistically an entire day is recommended. The gardens are in bloom most of the year, with spring being the peak season for azaleas and winter, the best time for camellias. If you plan to visit in summer, remember to bring the insect repellent. Most of the gardens are accessible to the handicapped. Some assistance may be needed for gravel pathways.

Middleton Place

Ashley River Road
Charleston, South Carolina 29414-7206
803-556-6020   or   800-782-3608

HISTORY

*M*iddleton Place is home to America's oldest landscaped gardens. Landscaping of the plantation's signature Butterfly Lakes and Terraces was begun in 1741 by Henry Middleton. It took one hundred slaves nearly ten years of steady labor to complete the project. Henry Middleton, the original owner of the plantation, was president of the First Continental Congress, and his son, Arthur, was a signer of the Declaration of Independence.

The original house was constructed in the 1740s, with north and south flanking wings added later. Looted and burned by a New York volunteer detachment of General William T. Sherman's army on February 22, 1865, less than one month before the end of the Civil War, the main house and south wing were destroyed. The north wing, built in 1755 as gentlemen's guest quarters, was not as severely damaged and was restored in the 1870s by Williams Middleton. In 1886, an earthquake leveled the ruins of the main house and south wing. The plantation's gardens and gentlemen's guest quarters, now designated a National Historic Site, were opened to the public in 1975.

HOURS

Daily, 9:00 a.m. to 5:00 p.m.

FEE

Yes, some discounts may apply

SIZE

110 acres on the Ashley River

FEATURES

The gardens are more than 250 years old and are spectacular anytime of the year due to Charleston's moderate climate. Middleton Place possesses the symmetry that is characteristic of European design of seventeenth-century gardens. The design elements in the garden are artfully executed with native lowcountry plants and exotic imports. Azaleas blanket the hillsides near the Rice Mill Pond, and camellias, roses, crepe myrtles, and magnolias lend an air of southern elegance to the landscape. Other features include Middleton Place House, which displays family treasures from the 1740s through the 1880s. Also, there is the plantation stable yard which offers a glimpse of the activities that helped to sustain lowcountry plantation life for more than a hundred years.

Japanese wisteria, azaleas, and dogwoods reflect in the dark waters beneath the bridge over the Rice Mill Pond.

Azaleas peek through the pickets of a moss-covered fence.

*Ancient live oak trees with their gnarled limbs
line the pathways of Middleton Place.*

DIRECTIONS

From I-26 take Exit 216A (SC 7 South) and follow the historic plantation signs on Rittenburg Boulevard to SC 61. Turn right onto SC 61 North (Ashley River Road). The plantation will be on the right at 17 miles. Middleton Place is located just north of Magnolia Plantation and Gardens.

A solitary horse gazes from the barn door into the plantation's stable yard.

Mute swans glide slowly across the surface of the fog-shrouded Rice Mill Pond.

TIPS

Children will love the stable yard with all the animals and the craftsmen. History buffs can immerse themselves in Middleton Place House, and gardening enthusiasts will be in heaven. The gardens have two peak blooming seasons: spring, for the azaleas; and winter, for the camellias. A variety of the other plants keep the gardens in color throughout the summer. Most of the grounds are accessible to the handicapped.

South Carolina Botanical Garden

Department of Horticulture
P.O. Box 340375
Clemson, South Carolina 29634-0375
803-656-3405

HISTORY

*B*eginning serendipitously in 1958, when camellias were transplanted to a plot on John C. Calhoun's Fort Hill estate, the South Carolina Botanical Garden has grown into a resource garden used and enjoyed by thousands of visitors. Initially called the Horticultural Gardens of Clemson University, the name was changed in 1987 to the Clemson University Botanical Garden. A final name was bestowed on the garden by the general assembly in 1992. Now known as the South Carolina Botanical Garden, its supporters were ecstatic at finally having formal designation as the state's first botanical garden.

HOURS

Daily, sunrise to sunset

FEE

None

SIZE

256 acres

FEATURES

This garden has features to satisfy any horticultural preference, including the Camellia Collection, the Bernice Dodgens Lark Wildflower Meadow, the Woodland Wildflower Trail, the Flower and Turf Display Garden, the Miller Dwarf Conifer Garden, the Xeriscape Garden, the Meditation Garden, the Marsh and Bog Habitat, and the Braille Trail. There is also a LISA (low impact sustainable agriculture) demonstration vegetable garden and a pioneer complex.

DIRECTIONS

From I-85 take Exit 19B at US 76 West. Travel approximately 11 miles. Turn left onto Perimeter Road and the garden will be on the left.

TIPS

There is much to see and do at this garden. Guided nature walks, a horticultural lecture series, and the Daffodil Festival are held during the year. Some areas are handicapped accessible.

Purple and white globe amaranth blanket the ground with color in the Flower and Turf Display Garden.

Boylston Gardens

Governor's Mansion
800 Richland Street
Columbia, South Carolina 29201-2397
803-737-1710

HISTORY

*B*oylston Gardens is part of a three-mansion complex known as the Governor's Green. It is located behind the Caldwell-Boylston House which was built in 1830. Surrounded by elaborate fencing and huge iron gates, the gardens, designed as an outdoor cathedral, were planted by Sarah Smith Boylston. Later, she donated part of the garden to the Garden Club of South Carolina to be used as a memorial to those who fought and died in World War II.

The Governor's Mansion, situated on the lion's share of the property, was built in 1855 by the Arsenal Military Academy to lodge their officers. It has served as the governor's mansion since 1868. The Lace House, built in 1854, is the other house in the complex. It is distinguished by the decorative ironwork which gives it the appearance of being trimmed in lace.

HOURS

Monday through Friday
9:30 a.m. to 4:30 p.m.

FEE

None

SIZE

9 acres in the historic district

FEATURES

The gardens of the Lace House and the Caldwell-Boylston House have been restored and feature a rose garden, fountains, patterned flower beds, secluded gardens, and beautiful tree-lined pathways. One of the newest and most popular features is the wedding garden. There is also a gift shop on the grounds.

DIRECTIONS

From I-20 take Exit 64A (I-26 East/US 76). This becomes Elmwood Avenue. At 3.8 miles, turn right onto Lincoln Street. Go two blocks to Richland Street. The gardens are at the corner of Richland and Lincoln streets.

TIPS

Reservations for tours of Boylston Gardens must be made at least one week in advance. Allow two hours to tour the complex. The gardens are handicapped accessible.

Memorial Garden

Garden Club of South Carolina
c/o Mrs. Herbert A. Wood
1107 Jessamine Street
Cayce, South Carolina 29033-4329
803-796-6446

HISTORY

*I*n 1944, the Garden Club of South Carolina decided to establish a garden honoring the servicemen who fought and died in World War II. A search committee was formed to locate an affordable piece of property. When no appropriate parcel could be located, a member of the search committee, Sarah Smith Boylston, offered to donate the rear portion of her existing garden.

Her generous offer was accepted by the member garden clubs, and in 1945, the Memorial Garden was established. A master plan for the garden was developed and donated by Charleston landscape architect, Loutrel A. Briggs. Funding was obtained from the state legislature for planting and maintenance.

HOURS

Sunday, 1:00 p.m. to 5:00 p.m.
except during extreme weather conditions

FEE

None

SIZE

¼ acre

FEATURES

Heavy iron gates open into a tiny garden sanctuary artfully planted with boxwoods, star magnolias, camellias, dogwoods, and a variety of evergreens. This quiet place offers the visitor a cozy atmosphere shielded from the bustle of activity in Columbia and the nearby Boylston Gardens. The garden, located at the rear of the Caldwell-Boylston House and its gardens, is completely fenced, which adds to the air of tranquility.

DIRECTIONS

From I-20 take Exit 64A (I-26 East/US 76). This becomes Elmwood Avenue. At 3.8 miles, turn right onto Lincoln Street. Travel one block. The garden is at the corner of Lincoln and Calhoun streets.

TIPS

This is a small garden with limited hours and may be visited in conjunction with the many other gardens and historic homes in Columbia. The garden is accessible to the handicapped.

Crepe myrtles and old roses are bordered by neatly clipped boxwood hedges in Founder's Garden at Robert Mills House.

Robert Mills House

1616 Blanding Street
Columbia, South Carolina 29201-3440
803-252-1770

HISTORY

One of the few residences designed by Robert Mills, designer of the Washington Monument, this home is now a decorative arts museum. It was originally designed in 1823 for Ainsley Hall, a wealthy Columbia merchant who died before the house was completed. The property was purchased by the Presbyterian Theological Seminary and used for religious activities until 1961.

Threatened with demolition in 1961, Robert Mills House was saved through the efforts of preservationists who have painstakingly restored the house and grounds. Restoration was aided by Mills's manuscripts and historical survey documents.

HOURS

Grounds
Daily, sunrise to sunset
House
Tuesday through Saturday
10:15 a.m. to 3:15 p.m.
Sunday
1:15 p.m. to 4:15 p.m.

FEE

Grounds are free, fee charged to tour house

SIZE

4 acres

FEATURES

Authentically restored grounds boast the Founder's Garden and expanses of lawn designed to showcase the house. Native plants, crepe myrtles, roses, magnolia trees, and large clipped hedges create an appropriate landscape for a home of the early 1800s.

DIRECTIONS

From I-20 take Exit 64A (I-26 East/US 76). This becomes Elmwood Avenue. At 4.5 miles, turn right onto Assembly Street. Go 4 blocks and turn left onto Blanding Street. The house is at 1616 Blanding.

TIPS

If you intend to visit the house consider taking the historical homes tour offered by the Richland County Historic Preservation Commission. It includes several historical houses of note in the Columbia area. The grounds are accessible to the handicapped.

Horseshoe at the University of South Carolina

University of South Carolina
Visitor Center-Carolina Plaza
937 Assembly Street
Columbia, South Carolina 29201-3937
803-777-8161

HISTORY

The Horseshoe at the University of South Carolina is the original campus of the university. Chartered in 1801 as South Carolina College, the university will soon celebrate its two hundredth anniversary. As the Fighting Gamecocks make their way into the twenty-first century, they are remembering and preserving their past. There are eleven buildings standing on the Horseshoe—a National Historic Place—and all, except for the McKissick Museum, were built during the early to mid-nineteenth century. All ten of these historic structures have been restored to their original appearance and are still in use by the university. Renovations to these historic buildings began in the 1970s, and it was during this time that the gardens were added on the grounds. There are five gardens; however, the President's House Garden is not open to the public. The gardens open to the public

are the Rose Garden at Lieber College, the Sundial Garden just to the east of Rutledge College, McCutchen House Gardens, and the Caroliniana Garden located behind the South Caroliniana Library.

HOURS

Daily, sunrise to sunset

FEE

None

SIZE

Campus quadrangle covering 4 city blocks

FEATURES

Each of the four gardens add their own charm to an already charming setting. The gardens are tucked behind and beside beautiful old buildings located along the edge of the Horseshoe. At the head of the Horseshoe is the McKissick Museum. The Sundial Garden is located to the right of the museum and adjacent to Rutledge College. This small garden has been recently restored by Omicron Delta Kappa in honor of its members and

The Caroliniana Garden, behind the South Caroliniana Library, is one of the gardens located around the Horseshoe.

Benches, surrounded by brick walls in the Lieber Rose Garden, provide the perfect place to study or reflect.

alumni. To the left of the museum is DeSaussure College and McCutchen House. The McCutchen Garden is located between the two buildings. Crepe myrtle trees, Bradford pears, camellias, azaleas, and seasonal annuals are featured in this garden. The other two gardens are located behind the two buildings which form the base of the Horseshoe, Lieber College and the South Caroliniana Library. The Lieber Rose Garden, funded by the Columbia Garden Club, honors deceased garden club members with roses, crepe myrtles, and Indian hawthorn. The Caroliniana Garden, restored largely through the efforts of Mrs. Edmund Taylor, former president of the University of South Caroliniana Society, is planted with gardenias, azaleas, nandinas, magnolias, and a Japanese maple. A large, three-tiered fountain at the Caroliniana Garden is dedicated to the memory of "The Carolina Patriots who fought in the American Revolution."

Gnarled branches of bushivy lean against an old brick wall in the Horseshoe at the University of South Carolina.

DIRECTIONS

From I-20 take Exit 64-A (I-26 East/US 76). This becomes Elmwood Avenue. At 4.5 miles, turn right onto Assembly Street. Travel eleven blocks and turn left onto Pendleton Street. Go two blocks to Sumter Street and turn right. The Horseshoe is on the left in the middle of the block.

TIPS

The gardens are accessible to the handicapped and parking is available on the street. Other gardens on campus include the Alumni House Garden, the Gibbes Green, behind the McKissick Museum, and the Moore Garden behind the South Tower. Belser Arboretum is located 2.4 miles from campus on Bloomwood Road.

Henry Timrod Park

City of Florence Parks Division
City County Complex RR
180 North Irby Street
Florence, South Carolina 29501-3456
803-665-3270

HISTORY

*N*amed for Henry Timrod (1828-1867), the poet laureate of the Confederacy, the park was established in 1925 from property donated to the city of Florence by a group of citizens interested in setting aside a part of their neighborhood for use as a park. Henry Timrod Park is a multipurpose recreational area, which is part of a twelve-park system totaling more than 180 acres. It is at Henry Timrod Park that the Florence Rotary Club's Beauty Trail begins and ends.

The Beauty Trail, established in 1946, was a Rotary Club public service project initiated by Charles Womack, president of the club from 1946-47. Womack worked with city officials and the public to showcase the park system and the lovely old neighborhoods. In order to display the more colorful areas of Florence, the trail route is changed every few years as the neighborhoods' landscape changes.

HOURS

Daily, sunrise to sunset

FEE

None

SIZE

18 acres

FEATURES

The park is primarily a recreational facility offering lighted tennis courts, picnic areas, a wheelchair fitness trail, a playground, formal gardens, and a gazebo. Other features include a tree identification trail and the one-room schoolhouse of Henry Timrod.

DIRECTIONS

From I-95 take Exit 160A (I-20 Business/David McLeod Boulevard) and travel 1.9 miles. Turn left onto Palmetto Street (US 76 East). At 1.8 miles, turn right onto Park Avenue, and at 0.4 mile, turn left onto Spruce Street. Timrod Park will be on the right at 0.1 mile.

TIPS

The Florence Museum is right next door to the park. Most areas of the park are handicapped accessible.

Lucas Park

City of Florence Parks Division
City County Complex RR
180 North Irby Street
Florence, South Carolina 29501-3456
803-665-3253

HISTORY

*L*ucas Park is a neighborhood nature garden established in the mid-1960s. The park is named for Florence businessman Marion D. Lucas, president of Florence Trust Company. Planning for the park began in 1954, when landscape architect Harold C. Weldon was engaged to develop a plan. It wasn't until 1961, when the park received an Aiken Foundation grant, that the master plan was executed. The grant allowed for the planting of more than thirteen thousand camellias and azalea.

Lucas Park is one of the stops on the ten-mile Beauty Trail which winds through the established neighborhoods of Florence. The trail is an on-going project of the Rotary Club and incorporates other parks in Florence, including Jeffries Creek Park, the largest of the city's parks, and Charlie Womack Park, named for the man responsible for establishing the Beauty Trail.

HOURS

Daily, sunrise to sunset

FEE

None

SIZE

12 acres

FEATURES

Dogwood, cherry, and redbud trees start the spring show and are followed by azaleas, wisteria, tulips, and jasmine. The park offers recreational facilities, a playground, and a picnic area.

DIRECTIONS

From I-95 take Exit 160A (I-20 Business/David McLeod Boulevard) and travel 1.9 miles. Turn left onto Palmetto Street (US 76 East). At 1.8 miles, turn right onto Park Avenue, and at 0.9 mile, Lucas Park will be on the left.

TIPS

This neighborhood park should be toured as part of the Beauty Trail. The surrounding well-planted homes add to the colorful springtime display. Accessibility for the handicapped is limited.

Hopsewee Plantation

Route 2, Box 205
Georgetown, South Carolina 29440-9232
803-546-7891

HISTORY

Hopsewee was home to Thomas Lynch, Sr. and Thomas Lynch, Jr., the only father and son to serve in the Continental Congress. The elder Lynch named the plantation by combining two words from the Cherokee and the Sewee Sioux living in the area. In the 1730s, the principal Indian chief for the Cherokee was Kana gato-ga, Cherokee for "Standing Turkey." The white men who knew him called him "Old Hop." At this same time, a band of Sewee Sioux lived along the Santee River. Sewee is Sioux for "island." Built of black cypress around 1740, Hopsewee, a National Historic Landmark, has been owned by only four families. Virtually unchanged since its construction, the house is flanked by two cypress-shingled outbuildings that served as kitchens.

HOURS
Grounds
Daily, sunrise to sunset
House
Tuesday through Friday
10:00 a.m. to 4:00 p.m.

FEE

Yes

SIZE

75 acres on the North Santee River

FEATURES

A woodland trail and the North Santee River offer beauty and a quiet place for reflection. The house is surrounded by live oak trees dripping with gray-green Spanish moss. The woodland trail, which winds through a forest of live oak, pine, and some hardwoods, is of special interest to nature lovers. Native plants predominate the landscape, which is a re-creation of the plantation landscape of the South Carolina lowcountry.

DIRECTIONS

Hopsewee is located 12 miles south of Georgetown on US 17 on the North Santee River. Historical markers along the highway make the plantation easy to find.

TIPS

The camellias bloom from October to April. During the summer months, bring mosquito repellent if you plan to spend time along the woodland trail.

Park Seed Trial and Display Garden

Cokesbury Road
Greenwood, South Carolina 29647-0001
803-223-7333

HISTORY

In 1868, sixteen-year-old George W. Park began a mail-order seed business using seeds he had saved from his own garden and an eight-page "catalogue" of his own design. In just a few years, his business became a success; but George wanted to know more about the seeds he was selling. In 1882, using money earned from his business, he entered Michigan State University where he earned a degree in horticulture.

After college, he returned home to his business in Pennsylvania; but the climate wasn't conducive to providing his customers with the widest variety of available plants. So, he moved the business, eventually settling in Greenwood. Here the business and his family life blossomed. George Park died in 1935; but Mary, his widow, and two sons, George Barratt and William, continued with the family business. Park Seed Company is still owned and operated by members of the Park Family.

HOURS

Daily, sunrise to sunset

FEE

None

SIZE

9 acres

FEATURES

Seventeen demonstration gardens planted with various species of annuals, perennials, vegetables, shrubs, roses, herbs, bulbs, and trees surround the Park Seed facility.

DIRECTIONS

From I-26 take Exit 54 (SC 72) south. SC 72 becomes SC 72/US 221 before entering the town. At the junction of SC 72/US 221 (Reynolds Avenue) and SC 254 (Grace Avenue), turn right. Park Seed Company is 6 miles north of Greenwood on SC 254.

TIPS

The last Saturday in June is when "Flower Day" is held. This also happens to be when summer annuals are at their peak. Individuals and small groups are easily accommodated; however, large groups should call ahead. The gardens are handicapped accessible.

Francis Beidler Forest

336 Sanctuary Road
Harleyville, SC 29448-3324
803-462-2150

HISTORY

Francis Beidler was a lumberman ahead of his time. He is responsible for saving the only virgin bald cypress and tupelo gum forest left in the world. He saved it from the saws and axes that were his livelihood. Beidler gained his appreciation for nature in 1875 while on vacation at what is now Yellowstone National Park. Beidler had heard outlandish stories of a strange and wonderful area in Wyoming, so he set out with a guide and several pack horses to investigate this unusual place. Beidler was awe-struck at the natural beauty of the area. Inspired by President Teddy Roosevelt's initiative to preserve this beautifully unusual land and by Gifford Pinchot's advocacy of conservation through wise use of public lands, Beidler began to champion the cause of preservation of our natural beauty in the United States, particularly in South Carolina.

Although Francis Beidler died in 1924, his family continued to preserve his land holdings in South Carolina's Four Hole Swamp. In the late 1960s, the estate was to be liquidated and the threat of logging loomed over the forest. The prospect of losing such an irreplaceable part of our natural heritage prompted the National Audubon Society and the Nature Conservancy to join forces. They purchased Beidler's forest and some of the surrounding wetlands and have preserved them for everyone to enjoy.

HOURS

Tuesday through Sunday
9:00 a.m. to 5:00 p.m.
Closed Mondays,
Thanksgiving, Christmas Eve, Christmas Day,
New Year's Eve, and New Year's Day

FEE

Yes. Children under six and
Audubon Life Members admitted free

SIZE

5,820 acres

FEATURES

This is a virgin forest with trees that are at least one thousand years old. A one-and-one-half-mile boardwalk winds through the black water swamp, giving the visitor the opportunity for a first-hand experience with unspoiled nature. A visitor center with exhibits and displays helps prepare you for your wilderness walk .

Ancient bald cypress and the wild creatures which live in Beidler Forest can be seen from the boardwalk.

DIRECTIONS

From I-26 West take Exit 187, turn left onto SC 27 and go to US 78. Turn right onto US 78 and go to US 178. Follow the signs to the sanctuary. From I-26 East take Exit 177, turn right onto SC 453 and go to US 178. Turn left onto US 178 and go through Harleyville. Follow the signs from the edge of town to the sanctuary.

TIPS

While on the boardwalk, stop and listen for the multitude of wildlife living in the forest. Benches are provided for resting or observing. Camping is not allowed in the sanctuary, and there are no food facilities. Pets are prohibited on the boardwalk. The visitor center and boardwalk are handicapped accessible.

Kalmia Gardens of Coker College

1624 West Carolina Avenue
Hartsville, South Carolina 29550-4906
803-383-8145

HISTORY

*O*nce the prosperous plantation of Thomas Edward Hart in the eighteenth century, the property, known as Laurel Land, fell into disrepair until it was acquired by Dr. William C. Coker in the early 1930s. Dr. Coker, busy with projects in Chapel Hill, North Carolina, gave the overgrown and neglected property to his sister-in-law, May Roper Coker. Miss May, as she was known to the citizens of Hartsville, was an avid gardener equal to the task of revitalizing Laurel Land. Her garden project quickly became known as "Miss May's Folly."

Overcoming the hurdles of skepticism and the Great Depression, Miss May created a public garden paradise. In 1935, she opened Kalmia Gardens, named for the mountain laurel (*Kalmia latifolia*) growing wild along the banks of the Black Creek. Miss May donated the gardens to Coker College in 1965 as a memorial to her husband, David Robert Coker.

HOURS

Daily, sunrise to sunset

FEE

None

SIZE

30 acres

FEATURES

Mountain laurel fills the gardens with clusters of tiny white blooms. Other flowering shrubs, such as azaleas and camellias, add to the natural beauty of the laurel thickets. Garden trails include the Camellia Trail, the Bluff Trail and the Bog Garden Trail.

DIRECTIONS

From I-20 take Exit 116 (US 15) to Hartsville. In downtown Hartsville, take SC Business 151 West (West Carolina Avenue) 2.6 miles to the gardens.

TIPS

Go to the gardens in May to enjoy the mountain laurel. Handicapped individuals will require assistance.

Azaleas bloom along the trails that weave through Kalmia Gardens.

Shady paths wind through the woods at Kalmia Gardens.

*A bench surrounded by colorful blooms makes
for an inviting place to stop and rest.*

Cypress Gardens

3030 Cypress Gardens Road
Moncks Corner, South Carolina   29461-6406
803-553-0515

HISTORY

Cypress Gardens, now a moss-covered paradise, was originally part of Dean Hall Plantation, one of the most prosperous rice plantations along the Cooper River. The first house at the plantation, Nesbitt House, was built about 1725 by Sir Alexander Nesbitt of Dean, Scotland. Almost one hundred years later, William Carson built Dean Hall. Both houses were moved from the property years ago.

In 1909, the plantation was purchased by Benjamin R. Kittredge for his wife, a lowcountry native. Dean Hall provided Mrs. Kittredge with a winter retreat surrounded by familiar scenery and Mr. Kittredge with prime duck hunting.

Legend has it that the inspiration for the gardens came when Mr. Kittredge saw the reflection of a red maple leaf in the black swamp water.

HOURS

Daily, 9:00 a.m. to 5:00 p.m.

FEE

Yes

SIZE

162 acres

FEATURES

Cypress Gardens, with water lilies and cattails growing along the edge of a swamp, are unique. The gardens feature the Azalea Garden, the Wedding Garden, the Butterfly Garden, the Woodland Garden, the Garden of Memories, and the Camellia Garden. The gardens can be seen from two vantage points. Footpaths meander through the gardens for more than three miles. However, the more interesting way to see the gardens is by flat-bottomed boat. You may paddle yourself or opt for the guided tour. The boat tour offers sights rarely seen from the shore.

DIRECTIONS

From I-26 take the US 52/Moncks Corner Exit. Take US 52 past Goose Creek and follow signs to Cypress Gardens Road (right).

TIPS

Beginning in February and continuing through the summer, the forest is filled with thousands of bulbs and other flowering plants. Handicapped parking is available.

Searching for their place in the sun, white water lilies emerge and dot the black water of Cypress Gardens swamp.

Nancy Bryan Luce Gardens at Mepkin Abbey

Highway Contract Route 69, P. O. Box 800
Moncks Corner, South Carolina 29461-9722
803-761-8509

HISTORY

*T*he Indian translation for Mepkin is believed to be "serene and lovely," which perfectly describes this plantation originally owned by Henry Laurens, the first president of the Continental Congress. Laurens, who died in 1792, is buried at Mepkin along with other members of his family. Like other plantations, Mepkin was passed down through the family for generations before it was eventually sold. Mepkin was purchased by publisher and philanthropist Henry Robinson Luce and his wife, dramatist Claire Boothe Luce. They used the property as a summer home until 1949, when a large portion of the plantation was donated to the Cistercian-Trappist Monks, who turned it into a monastery. This particular Catholic order of monks leads a simple life devoid of material assets; however, they do not prohibit involvement with the outside world and welcome visitors.

Named for Nancy Bryan Luce, the wife of Henry R. Luce III, the gardens located on the grounds of the monastery are terraced into a gently rolling hillside. Ponds, which provide a haven for waterfowl, flow into the nearby Cooper River.

HOURS

Daily, 9:00 a.m. to 4:30 p.m.

FEE

None

SIZE

5 acres

FEATURES

Nestled in pine woodlands along the west bank of the Cooper River, the Nancy Bryan Luce Gardens offer a variety of native plants, camellias, azaleas, tea olives, and dogwoods, as well as ancient live oak trees perpetually adorned with Spanish moss. The grounds are alive with wildlife native to the South Carolina lowcountry and the wetlands nourished by the river are home to a variety of plants and animals. The most notable feature, for some, is the hospitality of the monks.

The gently sloping terraces of Nancy Bryan Luce Gardens at Mepkin Abbey are filled with native plants.

DIRECTIONS

From I-26 take Exit 199 (US 17 Alternate). Go through Moncks Corner and cross the Cooper River. At 0.3 mile, on the other side of the bridge, turn right onto SC 402. At 2 miles, cross the Waboo Bridge and take an immediate right onto River Road. The entrance to the abbey is on the right at 6 miles.

TIPS

The gardens at Mepkin Abbey are open year round; however, they are at their colorful peak from late March to the first weeks of April. Upon your arrival at the reception center, ring the bell to summon the guestmaster. The gardens are accessible to the handicapped, with assistance required in some areas.

Brookgreen Gardens

1931 Brookgreen Gardens Drive
Murrells Inlet, South Carolina 29576-5101
803-237-4218

HISTORY

*R*ailroad heir Archer M. Huntington and his wife, Anna Hyatt Huntington, vacationed in the South Carolina lowcountry. When Anna's health required a milder climate, the area became the ideal place for a new home. In January 1930, the Huntingtons purchased four plantations: Brookgreen, The Oaks, Springfield, and Laurel Hill. They called their new home Brookgreen.

The varied history of the original property known as Brookgreen began in the 1700s when it was settled by the Allston family. In the early 1800s, Brookgreen was owned by Joshua Ward, who ran it as a rice plantation. When rice was no longer profitable, he turned to growing indigo. The Civil War devastated the colonial economy, forcing many plantation owners to either sell or abandon their properties. In 1870, Brookgreen was acquired by Dr. Louis Hasell, whose family lived there for a number of years. Subsequent owners used the property as a hunting reserve. After the Huntingtons purchased the property, it began to reach its full potential.

Drawing on her artistic talents as a sculptress, Anna Huntington formulated, designed, and executed the twofold, original garden plan. The first, and most important, aspect of the plan was to preserve and protect the wonderful natural treasures. Her plan was to enhance the already beautiful native flora with additional plantings suitable to the area. The second part of the plan was designed to showcase her massive pieces of sculpture. This part of the plan evolved to include the work of other American sculptors in the garden displays.

In 1931, Archer M. Huntington established Brookgreen Gardens, a Society for the Southeastern Flora and Fauna. He transferred Brookgreen into an eleemosynary corporation, which would effectively keep the gardens intact and used for the purpose he and his wife intended.

HOURS

Daily, 9:30 a.m. to 4:45 p.m.
Grounds are cleared at 5:30 p.m.
Closed Christmas

FEE

Yes, some discounts may apply

Pegasus by Laura Garden Fraser, carved from Mount Airy granite, rises from its base.

Located in the Center Garden, Pastoral *by Edmond R. Amateis is enhanced by its colorful surroundings.*

SIZE

9,127 acres from the Atlantic Ocean to the Waccamaw River in Georgetown County

FEATURES

One of the finest collections of American figurative sculpture assembled in one of the premier gardens in the Southeast, Brookgreen Gardens is, as Archer M.

Huntington said, "a quiet joining of hands between science and art." More than five hundred pieces of sculpture representing nineteenth- and twentieth-century artists such as Frederic Remington, Carl Milles, Daniel Chester French, and Anna Hyatt Huntington are displayed amid the trees and shrubs. Man-made metals and deliberately carved stone are enhanced by lines and colors artfully produced by Mother Nature, whose work is also on display.

The gardens are designed as a butterfly. The wing segments are "garden rooms" used as outdoor galleries. Other gardens include the Live Oak Allée, the Palmetto Garden, The Fountain of the Muses, and the South Carolina Terrace. Other features include the twenty-three-acre Wildlife Park, the Plantation Kitchen, the Small Sculpture Gallery, the Education Center, and a Museum Shop. The property is also a wildlife refuge.

DIRECTIONS

The gardens are located 18 miles south of Myrtle Beach on US 17 South. The entrance is directly across from Huntington Beach State Park.

TIPS

The favorable climate of South Carolina's lowcountry keeps the gardens of Brookgreen in almost perpetual color. Various species of flowering plants, shrubs, and trees take their turn blooming from January through December; however, April to September represents the prime time for blooms. You can tour the various sculpture gardens by using a self-guided audio tape or joining a tour led by a knowledgeable volunteer. Or you may simply stroll the grounds at your leisure.

The Alligator Pool in the Center Garden has works like Herbert Adams's Sea Scape *perched on the rim of the pool.*

Programs on habitat preservation and lowcountry ecology are offered throughout the year. The gardens are accessible to the handicapped and wheechairs are available at the Visitors Pavilion. Picnicking facilities are on the grounds and the Terrace Café offers refreshments. The café is closed during the winter.

Youth Taming the Wild *is one of the many works of*
Anna Hyatt Huntington on display.

Karl Gruppe's Joy *is perfectly poised amid the azalea blossoms.*

Edisto Memorial Gardens

Orangeburg County Chamber of Commerce
250 John C. Calhoun Drive
Orangeburg, South Carolina 29116-0328
803-534-6821 or 803-533-6020

HISTORY

*L*ocated along the North Edisto River, the gardens began with five acres of azaleas in the early 1920s. Edisto Gardens, as it was originally called, is a city park that has grown to be one of South Carolina's most-visited gardens. In 1951, a rose garden was added to extend the blooming season. Planted with more than four thousand roses, the garden was designated an All-American Rose Selections display garden in 1973. The garden is one of twenty-three test sites in the country used by All-American Rose Selections to determine the hardiness of roses planted in various parts of the country.

In 1950, the gardens changed again with the addition of a large fountain. Erected as a memorial to soldiers who died in World Wars I and II, the Korean War, and the Vietnam conflict, the fountain prompted a name change for the gardens. Edisto Memorial Gardens, as it is now called, has more than four hundred thousand visitors each year.

HOURS

Daily, sunrise to sunset

FEE

None

SIZE

150 acres along the North Edisto River

FEATURES

Between March 15 and April 15, azaleas, dogwoods, and roses bloom beneath century-old cypress trees and towering old oaks. Recently, the gardens were expanded with the addition of the six-acre Horne Wetlands Park, accessible by over twenty-six-hundred feet of boardwalk. Other points of interest include a gazebo, a picnic area, a nature trail, a garden for the blind, and a boat dock for those interested in canoeing the North Edisto River. The Edisto River is the longest black water river in the world, running over two hundred miles. Each year, on the last full weekend in April, the gardens host the South Carolina Festival of Roses.

Bald cypress trees, surrounded by azaleas and dogwood trees, embrace one another in an idyllic garden setting.

DIRECTIONS

From either I-26 or I-95 take US 301 South to Orangeburg. The gardens are located on US 301 South (John C. Calhoun Drive) right behind the Orangeburg Chamber of Commerce.

TIPS

Self-guided tour booklets are available at the chamber of commerce office and the arts center located in the gardens. The wetlands park is accessible to the handicapped, as are most areas of the park.

Silvery Spanish moss hangs from the bald cypress trees like the tresses of an old southern lady.

Sweeping expanses of lawn provide a lush foundation for the vibrant colors in the Azalea Garden.

Glencairn Garden

P. O. Box 11706
155 Johnston Street
Rock Hill, South Carolina   29731-1706
803-329-5620

HISTORY

Glencairn Garden derives its name from Dr. David Bigger's ancestral home in Scotland. David and Hazel, his wife, began creating their private paradise in 1928 and formally opened it to the public in 1940. In order for future generations to enjoy the fruits of their labors, the Biggers deeded the property to the city of Rock Hill in 1958. This modern formal garden, designed by landscape architect Robert Marvin, is laced with winding trails leading through terraced lawns and banks of azaleas.

In the spring, Glencairn Garden is the focal point for Rock Hill's week-long "Come See Me" festival. At other times during the year, the garden hosts a variety of art shows, concerts, and other events.

HOURS

Daily, sunrise to sunset

FEE

None

SIZE

7½ acres

FEATURES

Thousands of azaleas (over forty varieties) form the horticultural base for this city garden. Rounding out the landscape are terraced lawns, magnolias, lilies, dogwoods, and beds of summer annuals. A cascading fountain flows into a reflecting pool complete with goldfish.

DIRECTIONS

From I-77 take Exit 82B and go west on Cherry Street approximately 4 miles. Turn left onto Charlotte Avenue and proceed 1 mile. Turn left onto Edgemont Avenue. Parking for the garden is along Edgemont Avenue.

TIPS

Azaleas and flowering trees make spring the perfect time to visit Glencairn Garden. Peak bloom is usually from middle to late April. The garden is handicapped accessible with suitable parking on Edgemont Avenue.

Water flows gently down the tiers of the Terrace Fountain towards the Lily Pond.

Hatcher Gardens

Spartanburg County Foundation
320 East Main Street
Spartanburg, South Carolina 29302-1943
803-582-2776

HISTORY

*T*n 1969, Harold Hatcher bought an eroded, abandoned cotton field overgrown with briars as a place to retire. He looked past the problems and saw only the possibilities. He envisioned a lush, tree-shaded garden complete with ponds, flowers, birds, and native wildlife.

Hatcher's mission was to transform an eyesore into an urban sanctuary where people could come to learn about landscaping and preserving the environment. Almost single-handedly, Hatcher and his wife began to turn a vision into reality. Piece by piece, more property was acquired. Eroded gullies were reshaped, and more than ten thousand plants were planted. As the property transformed and Mr. Hatcher aged, he realized the need to protect the urban haven he had created. In 1987, on his eightieth birthday, he donated the gardens to the city of Spartanburg along with an endowment. An additional agreement has arranged for the gardens to be maintained by the Spartanburg County Foundation created by the Men's Garden Club of Spartanburg.

HOURS

Daily, 9:00 a.m. to sunset

FEE

None

SIZE

7 acres

FEATURES

Native plants such as pawpaw, sweet bay magnolia, red buckeye, witch hazel, and strawberry bush provide the horticultural foundation for the gardens. Other plants include popular wildflowers like jack-in-the-pulpit, Virginia bluebell, and nodding trillium. An observation platform overlooks one of the many ponds in the gardens.

DIRECTIONS

From I-26 take Exit 22 (SC 296/Reidville Road) and travel east towards Spartanburg. At 1.8 miles, the gardens will be on the left at 820 Reidville Road.

TIPS

The time to visit these gardens is determined by your own particular horticultural interest. Wildflowers begin blooming in early spring, and various other plants continue the blooming cycle until late fall. Areas of the garden are handicapped accessible.

A golden northern bumblebee in search of pollen and nectar lands on a purple coneflower .

Summerville Azalea Park

Town of Summerville
104 Civic Center
Summerville, South Carolina 29483-6000
803-871-6000

HISTORY

The Works Progress Administration (WPA) in Dorchester County was headed by a Summerville resident, Herbert L. Bailey. In the 1930s, Bailey, with the help of Summerville mayor Grange Cuthbert and nurseryman George Segelken, began working to create a town park. Funds were secured through the WPA, and the local folks were put to work implementing the trio's plan to reclaim an area known as Pike's Hole.

Swampy land was drained, tangles of underbrush were cleared, and the gardens for the park were laid out. Thirty thousand azaleas, donated by Segelken, were planted. Summerville, with its new profusion of spring color, began to live up to its name of "Flowertown in the Pines." Beauty is fleeting, and over the next forty years, the park fell into disrepair—but not for long. Beth McIntosh, founder of the Summerville Preservation Society, suggested renewing the park as the town's bicentennial project. It took nearly a year; but the park, renewed and replanted, was more beautiful than ever.

HOURS

Daily, sunrise to sunset

FEE

None

SIZE

10 acres

FEATURES

Springtime azaleas, such as the "Pride of Summerville," are the highlight of the park. Plants featured at the park are camellias, water lilies, American chestnuts, azaleas, and various other flowering shrubs and trees. The park also features an amphitheater, a gazebo, several ponds, footbridges, paved pathways, and a picnic area.

DIRECTIONS

From I-26 take Exit 199A (US 17 Alternate) and travel south. At 1.8 miles, turn left onto East Richardson Avenue and travel 0.1 mile to South Magnolia Street, and turn right. Parking for the park is on the right at 0.3 mile.

TIPS

Parking is available on Azalea Street and South Main Street at the Cuthbert Community Center. Each spring, the Summerville YMCA sponsors the "Flowertown Festival." The park is handicapped accessible.

Fallen camellia blossoms cover the ground like a red velvet carpet.

Swan Lake Iris Gardens

P.O. Box 1449
Sumter, South Carolina 29151-1449
803-773-3371

HISTORY

"*B*eauty and the businessman" is a phrase which could start the story of Swan Lake Iris Gardens. Sumter businessman Hamilton Carr Bland was an avid gardener who wanted to surround his home with a variety of imported irises. In 1927, he planted and pampered the irises, but despite expert advice and constant care, the expected profusion of blooms never materialized. Disappointed in the performance of the plants, Bland ordered all of the irises to be uprooted and dumped in the marshy, low-lying area of the thirty-acre cypress swamp he had recently bought as a fishing retreat. The following spring, the edge of the swamp was in full bloom. Mr. Bland was delighted with this accidental success and began a plan to develop the property into a garden instead of a fishing retreat.

In 1938, A. T. Heath, another of Sumter's business leaders, deeded 120 acres across from Bland's swampy getaway to the city of Sumter. The donation carried the stipulation that the property was to be developed by Hamilton Carr Bland as part of the Swan Lake Iris Gardens. Mr. Bland deeded his gardens to the city in 1949. Since that time, the city has improved the gardens by adding more plants, pathways, a playground, tennis courts, and picnic tables.

HOURS

Daily, 8:00 a.m. to sunset

FEE

None

SIZE

150 acres, including 45 acres of lakes

FEATURES

The Kaempferi irises, better known as Japanese irises, bloom in the early summer and provide an extraordinary display of color that reflects in the dark, black waters of the lakes. Real and reflected colors of a variety of blooming plants such as azaleas, camellias, wisteria, magnolias, lotuses, water lilies, roses, and gardenias brighten the watery landscape. Throughout the gardens are the ever-present and always beautiful swans of Swan Lake. Introduced to the lakes by Mr. Bland before the irises were ever planted, the swans are the number one favorite attraction for all visitors. The gardens have seven of the eight known varieties of swans and hope to have all eight before the end of 1995.

Australian black swans are one of the seven swan species that live at Swan Lake Iris Gardens.

A Royal White Mute swan glides across the surface of the still waters of the lake.

Cypress tress and azaleas reflect in the waters of Swan Lake Iris Gardens.

DIRECTIONS

From I-95 take Exit 135 (US 378) towards Sumter. At 16 miles, take SC 763 (Myrtle Beach Highway) to East Liberty Street. Turn left onto East Liberty Street. At. 2.8 miles, the gardens will be on both sides of the street.

TIPS

The gardens host three festivals during the year, and admission to all festivals is free. Call or write for a brochure outlining festival activity and a blooming schedule for the gardens. The gardens are handicapped accessible.

Rose Hill Plantation State Park

2677 Sardis Road
Union, South Carolina 29201-7904
803-427-5966

HISTORY

William Henry Gist, the "Secession Governor of South Carolina," called Rose Hill Plantation home from 1832 until his death on September 30, 1874. The mansion was constructed from 1828 to 1832 on Gist's eight-thousand-acre cotton plantation. It was remodeled in the 1850s and the grounds were planted with roses circled by boxwoods. Rose Hill flourished under Gist's management; but, the Civil War changed everything.

Gist, governor of South Carolina at the outbreak of the war, voted to secede from the Union. After the war, he was pardoned by President Andrew Johnson after vowing loyalty to the United States. Gist died at Rose Hill, and his wife, Mary, continued to operate the farm, at that time one-fourth its original size, until her death in June 1889. After her death, Rose Hill was divided among the Gist grandchildren. The house fell into disrepair and the land lay fallow until the 1940s when the plantation was purchased by the Franks family of Laurens. The Franks, assisted by the Union County Daughters of the American Revolution, restored Rose Hill Plantation to its previous splendor. In December 1960, the state of South Carolina acquired the property and designated it as a state park.

HOURS

Grounds
Thursday through Monday
9:00 a.m. to 6:00 p.m.
Mansion
Saturday
10:00 a.m. to 3:00 p.m.
Sunday
12:00 p.m. to 3:00 p.m.
Other times by appointment

FEE

None

SIZE

44 acres

The Federal style mansion at Rose Hill Plantation was home to South Carolina's secession governor, William Gist.

FEATURES

Like most of South Carolina's state parks, Rose Hill Plantation State Park offers a variety of recreational facilities including picnic shelters, nature trails, and interpretive programs. Other features include the restored, nineteenth-century, Federal-style mansion filled with furnishings belonging to the Gist family. The rose garden, from which the plantation derives its name, is located adjacent to the mansion.

DIRECTIONS

From I-26 take Exit 44 (SC 49) towards the town of Union. Cross SC 56 and watch for the signs to the park. Turn right on Sardis Road and continue to the park.

TIPS

Picnic shelters require a reservation. The rose garden and grounds are accessible to the handicapped. Efforts are under way to further increase handicapped accessibility.

Silver Moon, a large-flowered climber, grows beside one of the plantation's support buildings.

The plantation rose garden is planted with many varieties of Old Garden roses such as Madam Hardy.

BIBLIOGRAPHY

Anderson, J. Jay. *North Wilkesboro: The First Hundred Years 1890-1990.* Charlotte, N.C.: Delmar Company, 1990.

Bache, Ellyn,et al., eds. *What Locals Know About Wilmington and Its Beaches.* Wilmington, N.C.: Banks Channel Books, 1993.

Buildings of the Columbia Campus: The University of South Carolina. Columbia, S. C.: Division of University Relations, 1990.

Chamberlin, Susan. *Hedges, Screens, and Espaliers: How to Select, Grow, and Enjoy.* Tucson, Ariz.: Horticultural Publishing, Co., Inc., 1983.

Dockstader, Frederick J. *Great North American Indians: Profiles in Life and Leadership.* New York: Van Nostrand Reinhold Company, 1977.

Graydon, Nell S., and Isabelle M. Hoogenboom. *South Carolina Gardens.* Beaufort, S.C.: Beaufort Book Company, 1973.

Harrington, J. C. *Archaeology and the Enigma of Fort Raleigh.* Raleigh, N.C.: Division of Archives and History, North Carolina Department of Cultural Resources, 1984.

Hewlett, Crockette W. *Between the Creeks: A History of Masonboro Sound 1735-1970.* By the author, 1971.

Hill, Barbara. "Park History is One of Renewal." *The Summerville Journal-Scene,* 30 March 1990, Flowertown Festival Section, p.2C.

_____. "Showplace is a Labor of Love." *The Summerville Journal-Scene,* 8 April 1994, p. 5A.

Maxey, Russell. *South Carolina's Historic Columbia: Yesterday and Today in Photographs.* Columbia, S.C.: R. L. Bryan Company, 1980.

Miller, Everitt L., and Jay S. Cohen. *The American Garden Guidebook.* New York: M. Evans and Company, Inc., 1987.

Page, Ralph W. *Flora Macdonald College: An Aftermath of History.* Charlotte, N.C.: Presbyterian Standard Publishing Company, 1916.

Ray, Mary Helen, and Robert P. Nicholls. *The Traveler's Guide to American Gardens.* Chapel Hill, N.C.: University of North Carolina Press, 1988.

Shaffer, E. T. H. *Carolina Gardens.* New York: Devin-Adair Company, 1939.

Travel Guide to Carolina Gardens. Greensboro, N.C.: Carolina Gardener Magazine, 1994.

Walker, Mrs. Archibald Wilson. *History of the Garden Club of South Carolina 1930-1950.* Spartanburg, S.C., n.d.

Waugh, Elizabeth Culbertson. *North Carolina's Capital: Raleigh.* Chapel Hill, N.C.: University of North Carolina Press, 1968.

Williams, Alexa Carroll, ed. *Raleigh: A Guide to North Carolina's Capital.* Raleigh, N.C.: Raleigh Fine Arts Society, Inc., 1975.

Wrenn, Tony. *Wilmington North Carolina: An Architectural and Historical Portrait.* Charlottesville, Va.: The University Press of Virginia, 1984.